Cybernetic Analysis for Stocks and Futures

Founded in 1807, John Wiley & Sons is the oldest independent publishing company in the United States. With offices in North America, Europe, Australia, and Asia, Wiley is globally committed to developing and marketing print and electronic products and services for our customers' professional and personal knowledge and understanding.

The Wiley Trading series features books by traders who have survived the market's ever changing temperament and have prospered—some by reinventing systems, others by getting back to basics. Whether a novice trader, professional, or somewhere in between, these books will provide the advice and strategies needed to prosper today and well into the future.

For a list of available titles, visit our Web site at www.WileyFinance.com.

Cybernetic Analysis for Stocks and Futures

Cutting-Edge DSP Technology to Improve Your Trading

JOHN F. EHLERS

WILEY

John Wiley & Sons, Inc.

Published by John Wiley & Sons, Inc., Hoboken, New Jersey.
Published simultaneously in Canada.

For general information on our other products and services, or technical support, please contact our Customer Care Department within the United States at 800-762-2974, outside the United States at 317-572-3993 or fax 317-572-4002.

Wiley also publishes its books in a variety of electronic formats. Some content that appears in print may not be available in electronic books.

For more information about Wiley products, visit our web site at www.wiley.com.

Library of Congress Cataloging-in-Publication Data:

Ehlers, John F., 1933-
   Cybernetic analysis for stocks and futures : cutting-edge DSP
technology to improve your trading / John F. Ehlers.
      p. cm.
Includes bibliographical references.
   ISBN 0-471-46307-8
   1. Corporations—Valuation.   2. Chief executive officers—Rating of.
3. Investment analysis.   I. Title.
HG4028.V3 E365 2004
332.63'2042—dc22   2003021212

10 9 8 7 6 5 4 3 2 1

*To Elizabeth—my friend,
my companion, my wife*

Acknowledgments

I would like to thank Mike Burgess, Rod Hare, and Mitchell Duncan, who took time out of their busy schedules to read and critique the early manuscripts of this book. Their efforts transformed the original terse descriptions of computer code and the often rambling musings and thought processes of an engineer into a readable document having a rational flow for you, the reader.

Tools are very important in our technological age. I would like to thank TradeStation Technologies for their platform, which made the development of trading systems possible. I would also like to thank eSignal for making their platform available for indicator development and Chris Kryza for converting my code to eSignal Formula Script. Additionally, I would like to thank Steve Ward, who made the resources of NeuroShell Trader available, thus enabling readers to extend the usefulness of my indicators by using neural networks and genetic algorithms.

I would also like to thank Mike Barna for showing me how to apply the coin toss methodology to trading strategy evaluation.

J. F. E.

Contents

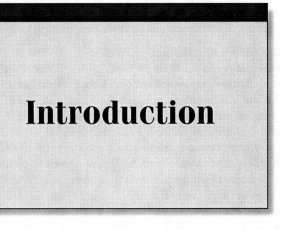

Introduction

"This is a synopsis of my book," Tom said abstractly.

As Sir Arthur C. Clarke has noted, any significantly advanced technology is indistinguishable from magic. The advances made in computer technology in the past two decades have been dramatic and can qualify as nearly magical. The computer on my desk today is far more powerful than that which was available to the entire national defense system just 30 years ago. Software for traders, however, has not kept pace. Most of the trading tools available today are neither different from nor more complex than the simple pencil-and-paper calculations that can be achieved through the use of mechanical adding machines. True, these calculations are now made with blinding speed and presented in colorful and eye-grabbing displays, but the power and usefulness of the underlying procedures have not changed. If anything, the relative power of the calculations has diminished because the increased speed of information exchange and increased market capitalization have caused fundamental shifts in the technical character of the market. These shifts include increased volatility and shorter periods for the market swings.

Cybernetic Analysis for Stocks and Futures promises to bring magic to the art of trading by introducing wholly new digital signal-processing techniques. The application of digital signal processing offers the advantage of viewing old problems from a new perspective. The new perspective gained by digital signal processing has led me to develop some profoundly effective new trading tools. The advances in trading tools, along with the continuing advancements in hardware capabilities, virtually ensure the continued application of digital signal processing in the future. Traders who master the new concepts, therefore, will find themselves at a great advantage when approaching the volatile market of the twenty-first century. If you like code, you will love this book. Every new technique, indicator, and automatic trading system is defined in exquisite detail in both EasyLanguage code for use in TradeStation and in eSignal Formula Script (EFS) code. They are also available as compiled DLLs to be run in NeuroShell trader.

Chapter 1 starts the wizardry off with a bang by challenging the conventional wisdom that market prices have a Gaussian probability density function (PDF). Just think about it. Do prices really have several events separated by a standard deviation from the mean across the screen as you would expect with a Gaussian PDF? Absolutely not! If the PDF is not Gaussian, then attaching significance to the one-sigma points in trading systems is, at best, just plain wrong. I show you how to establish an approximate Gaussian PDF through the application of the Fisher transform.

I derive a new zero-lag Instantaneous Trendline in Chapter 2. By dividing the market into a trend component and a cycle component, I create a zero-lag cycle oscillator from the derivation. These results are put to work by designing an automatic trend-following trading strategy in Chapter 3 and an automatic cycle-trading strategy in Chapter 4.

Several new oscillators are then derived. These include the CG Oscillator in Chapter 5 and the Relative Vigor Index (RVI) in Chapter 6. The performance of the Cyber Cycle Oscillator, the CG Oscillator, and the RVI are compared in Chapter 7. Noting that a favorite technical analysis tool is the Stochastic Relative Strength Index (RSI), where the RSI curve is sharpened by taking the Stochastic of it, I then show you in Chapter 8 how to enhance the oscillators by taking the Stochastic of them and also applying the Fisher transform.

In Chapter 9 I give an all-new exciting method of measuring market cycles. Using the Hilbert transform, a fast-reacting method of measuring cycles is derived. The validity and accuracy of these measurements are then demonstrated using several stressing theoretical waveforms. In Chapter 10 I then show you how to use the measured Dominant Cycle length to make standard indicators automatically adaptive to the measured Dominant Cycle. This adaptation makes good indicators stand out and sparkle as outstanding indicators. In Chapter 11, the cycle component of the Dominant Cycle is synthesized from the cycle measurement and displayed as the Sinewave Indicator. The advantages of the Sinewave Indicator are that it can anticipate cyclic turning points and that it is not subject to whipsaw trades when the market is in a trend. I continue the theme of adapting to the measured Dominant Cycle in Chapter 12 by showing you how to use the measurement to design an automatic trend-following trading strategy. The performance of the strategies I disclose is on par with or exceeds that of commercially available strategies.

Chapter 13 provides you with several types of filters that give vastly superior smoothing with a minimum penalty in lag. Computer code is provided for these filters, as well as tables of coefficient values. Another way to obtain superior smoothing is through the use of Laguerre polynomials. Laguerre polynomials enable smoothing to be done using a very short amount of data, as I explain in Chapter 14.

One of the problems with using backtests of automatic trading strategies is that they don't necessarily predict future performance. I describe a technique in Chapter 15 that will enable you to use the theory of probability to visualize how your trading strategy could perform. It also illustrates what historical parameters are important to make this assessment. In Chapter 16 I show you how to generate leading indicators, along with the penalty in increased noise that you must accept when these indicators are used. I conclude in Chapter 17 by showing you how to simplify the coding of simple moving averages (SMAs).

Many of the digital signal-processing techniques described in this book have been known and used in the physical sciences for many years. For example, Maximum Entropy Spectral Analysis (MESA) algorithm was originally developed by geophysicists in their exploration for oil. The small amount of data obtainable from seismic exploration demanded a solution using a short amount of data. I successfully adapted this approach and popularized it for the measurement of market cycles. More recently, the use of digital signal processing has exploded in consumer electronics, making devices such as CDs and DVDs possible. Today, complete radio receivers are constructed without the use of analog components. As we expand DSP use by introducing it to the field of trading, we will see that digital signal processing is an exciting new field, perfect for technically oriented traders. It allows us to generalize and expand the use of many traditionally used indicators as well as achieve more precise computations.

I begin each chapter with a Tom Swifty. Perhaps this is a testament to my adolescent sense of humor, but the idea is to anchor the concept of the chapter in your mind. A Tom Swifty is a play on words that follows an unvarying pattern and relies for its humor on a punning relationship between the way an adverb describes the speaker and at the same time refers significantly to the import of the speaker's statement, as in, *"I like fuzzy bunnies," said Tom acutely.* The combinations are endless. Since this book contains magic, perhaps I should have selected Harry Potter as a hero rather than Tom Swift.

Throughout this book my objective is to not only describe new techniques and tools but also to provide you the means to make your trading more profitable and therefore more pleasurable.

Cybernetic Analysis for Stocks and Futures

CHAPTER 1

The Fisher Transform

"I don't see any chance of a market recovery,"
said Tom improbably.

The focus of my research for more than two decades has been directed toward applying my background in engineering and signal processing to the art of trading. The goal of this book is to share the results of this research with you. Throughout the book I will demonstrate new methods for technical analysis of stocks and commodities and ways to code them for maximum efficiency and effectiveness. I will discuss methods for modeling the market to help categorize market activity. In addition to new indicators and automatic trading systems, I will explain how to turn good-performing traditional indicators into outstanding adaptive indicators. The trading systems that subsequently evolve from this analysis will seriously challenge, and often exceed, the consistent performance and profit-making capabilities of most commercially available trading systems. While much of what is covered in this book breaks new ground, it is not simply innovation for innovation's sake. Rather, it is intended to challenge conventional wisdom and illuminate the shortcomings of many prevailing approaches to systems development.

In this chapter we plunge right into an excellent example of challenging conventional wisdom. I know at least a dozen statistically based indicators that reference "the one-sigma point," "the three-sigma point," and so on. Sigma is the standard deviation from the mean. In order to have a standard deviation from the mean, one must know the probability density function (PDF). A Gaussian, or Normal, PDF is almost universally assumed. A Gaussian PDF is the familiar bell-shaped curve used to describe IQ distribution in the population and a host of other statistical descriptions. The Gaussian PDF has long "tails" that describe events that have a wide deviation from the mean with relatively low probability. With a Gaussian PDF, 68.26 percent of all occurrences fall within plus or minus one standard deviation from the mean, 95.44 percent of occurrences fall within plus or minus two standard deviations, and 99.73 percent of all occurrences fall within plus or minus three deviations. In other words, the majority of all cases fall within the one-sigma "boundary" with a Gaussian PDF. If an event falls outside the one-sigma level, then certain inferences have been drawn about what can happen in the future.

The real question here is whether the Gaussian PDF can be used to reliably describe market activity. You can easily answer that question yourself. Just think about the way prices look on a bar chart. Do you see only 68 percent of the prices clustered near the mean price? That is, do you see 32 percent of the prices separated by more than one deviation from the mean? And, do you see prices spike away from the mean nearly 5 percent of the time by two standard deviations? How often do you even see price spikes at all? If you don't see these deviations, a Gaussian PDF is not a good assumption.

The Fisher transform is a simple mathematical process used to convert any data set to a modified data set whose PDF is approximately Gaussian. Once the Fisher transform is computed, we can then analyze the transformed data set in terms of its deviation from the mean.

The Commodity Channel Index (CCI), developed by Donald Lambert, is an example of reliance on the Gaussian PDF assumption. The equation to compute the CCI is

$$CCI = \frac{Price - Moving\ Average}{0.015 * Deviation} \tag{1.1}$$

Deviation is computed from the difference of prices and moving average values over a period. The period of the moving average over which the computation is done is selectable by the user. The CCI can be viewed as the current deviation normalized to the standard deviation. But what gives with the 0.015 term? Well, conveniently enough, the reciprocal of 0.015 is 66.7, which is close enough to one standard deviation of a Gaussian PDF for most technical analysis work. The premise is that if prices exceed a standard deviation, they will revert to the mean. Therefore, the common rules are to sell if the CCI exceeds +100 and buy if the CCI is less than −100. Needless to say, the CCI can be improved substantially through the use of the Fisher transform.

Suppose prices behave as a square wave. If you tried to use the price crossing a moving average as a trading system, you would be destined for failure because the price has already switched to the opposite value by the time the movement is detected. There are only two price values. Therefore,

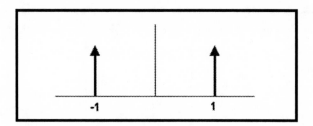

FIGURE 1.1   The Probability Distribution of a Square Wave Has Only Two Values

the probability distribution is 50 percent that the price will be at one value or the other. There are no other possibilities. The probability distribution of the square wave is shown in Figure 1.1. Clearly, this probability function does not remotely resemble a Gaussian probability distribution.

There is no great mystery about the meaning of a probability density or how it is computed. It is simply the likelihood the price will assume a given value. Think of it this way: Construct any waveform you choose by arranging beads strung on a series of parallel horizontal wires. After the waveform is created, turn the frame so the wires are vertical. All the beads will fall to the bottom, and the number of beads on each wire will stack up to demonstrate the probability of the value represented by each wire.

I used a slightly more sophisticated computer code, but nonetheless the same idea, to create the probability distribution of a sinewave in Figure 1.2. In this case, I used a total of 10,000 "beads." This PDF may be surprising, but if you stop and think about it, you will realize that most of the sampled data points of a sinewave occur near the maximum and minimum extremes. The PDF of a simple sinewave cycle is not at all similar to a Gaussian PDF. In fact, cycle PDFs are more closely related to those of a square wave. The high probability of a cycle being near the extreme values is one of the reasons why cycles are difficult to trade. About the only way to successfully trade a cycle is to take advantage of the short-term coherency and predict the cyclic turning point.

The Fisher transform changes the PDF of any waveform so that the transformed output has an approximately Gaussian PDF. The Fisher transform equation is

$$y = 0.5 * \ln \left[\frac{1+x}{1-x} \right]$$ (1.2)

Where x is the input
$\quad$ y is the output
$\quad$ ln is the natural logarithm

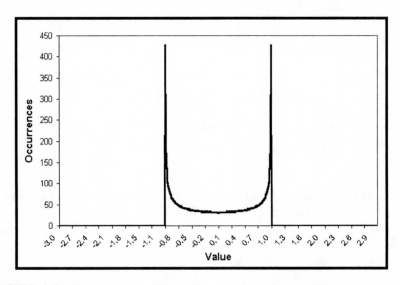

FIGURE 1.2   Sinewave Cycle PDF Does Not Resemble a Gaussian PDF

The transfer function of the Fisher transform is shown in Figure 1.3.

The input values are constrained to be within the range $-1 < X < 1$. When the input data is near the mean, the gain is approximately unity. For example, go to $x = 0.5$ in Figure 1.3. There, the Y value is only slightly larger than 0.5. By contrast, when the input approaches either limit within the

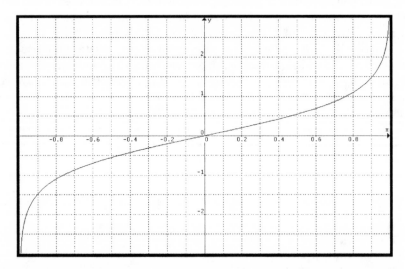

FIGURE 1.3   The Nonlinear Transfer of the Fisher Transform Converts Inputs (x Axis) to Outputs (y Axis) Having a Nearly Gaussian PDF

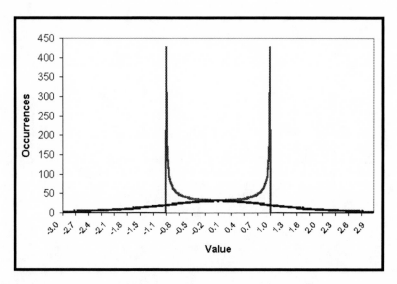

FIGURE 1.4 The Fisher-Transformed Sinewave Has a Nearly Gaussian PDF Shape

range, the output is greatly amplified. This amplification accentuates the largest deviations from the mean, providing the "tail" of the Gaussian PDF. Figure 1.4 shows the PDF of the Fisher-transformed output as the familiar bell-shaped curve, compared to the input sinewave PDF. Both have the same probability at the mean value. The transformed output PDF is nearly Gaussian, a radical change from the sinewave PDF.

I measured the probability distribution of U.S. Treasury Bond futures over a 15-year span from 1988 to 2003. To make the measurement, I created a normalized channel 10 bars long. The normalized channel is basically the same as a 10-bar Stochastic Indicator. I then measured the price location within that channel in 100 bins and counted up the number of times the price was in each bin. The results of this probability distribution measurement are shown in Figure 1.5. This actual probability distribution more closely resembles the PDF of a sinewave rather than a Gaussian PDF. I then increased the length of the normalized channel to 30 bars to test the hypothesis that the sinewave-like probability distribution is only a short-term phenomenon. The resulting probability distribution is shown in Figure 1.6. The probability distributions of Figures 1.5 and 1.6 are very similar. I will leave it to you to extend the probability analysis to any market of your choice. I predict you will get substantially similar results.

So what does this mean for trading? If the prices are normalized to fall within the range from −1 to +1 and subjected to the Fisher transform, extreme price movements are relatively rare events. This means the turning points can be clearly and unambiguously identified. The EasyLanguage

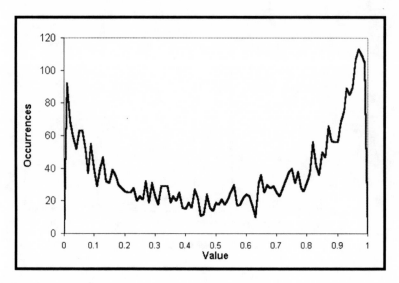

FIGURE 1.5   Probability Distribution of Treasury Bond Futures in a 10-Bar Channel over 15 Years

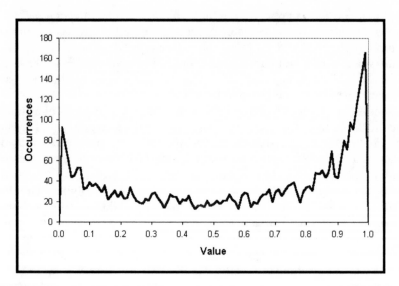

FIGURE 1.6   Probability Distribution of Treasury Bond Futures in a 30-Bar Channel over 15 Years

```
Inputs:      Price((H+L)/2),
             Len(10);

Vars:        MaxH(0),
             MinL(0),
             Fish(0);

MaxH = Highest(Price, Len);
MinL = Lowest(Price, Len);

Value1 = .5*2*((Price - MinL)/(MaxH - MinL) - .5)
   + .5*Value1[1];
If Value1 > .9999 then Value1 = .9999;
If Value1 < -.9999 then Value1 = -.9999;

Fish = 0.25*Log((1 + Value1)/(1 - Value1)) + .5*Fish[1];

Plot1(Fish, "Fisher");
Plot2(Fish[1], "Trigger");
```

FIGURE 1.7   EasyLanguage Code to Normalize Price to a 10-Day Channel and Compute Its Fisher Transform

code to do this is shown in Figure 1.7 and the eSignal Formula Script (EFS) code is shown in Figure 1.8. Value1 is a function used to normalize price within its last 10-day range. The period for the range is adjustable as an input. Value1 is centered on its midpoint and then doubled so that Value1 will swing between the −1 and +1 limits. Value1 is also smoothed with an exponential moving average whose alpha is 0.5. The smoothing may allow Value1 to exceed the 10-day price range, so limits are introduced to preclude the Fisher transform from blowing up by having an input value larger than unity. The Fisher transform is computed to be the variable "Fish". Both Fish and Fish delayed by one bar are plotted to provide a crossover system that identifies the cyclic turning points.

```
/************************************************************
Title:                    Fisher Transform
**********************************************************/

function preMain() {
    setStudyTitle("Fisher Transform");
    setCursorLabelName("Fisher", 0);
    setCursorLabelName("Trigger", 1);
    setDefaultBarFgColor(Color.blue, 0);
    setDefaultBarFgColor(Color.red, 1);
        setDefaultBarThickness(2, 0);
    setDefaultBarThickness(2, 1);
}

var Value1 = null;
var Value1_1 = 0;
var Fish = null;
var Fish_1 = 0;
var vPrice = null;
var aPrice = null;

function main(nLength) {
    var nState = getBarState();

        if (nLength == null) nLength = 10;
        if (aPrice == null) aPrice = new Array(nLength);

    if (nState == BARSTATE_NEWBAR && vPrice != null) {
      aPrice.pop();
      aPrice.unshift(vPrice);
      if (Value1 != null) Value1_1 = Value1;
      if (Fish != null) Fish_1 = Fish;
    }

        vPrice = (high() + low()) / 2;
        aPrice[0] = vPrice;

    if (aPrice[nLength-1] == null) return;

        var MaxH = high();
        var MinL = low();
        var temp;
```

FIGURE 1.8   EFS Code to Normalize Price to a 10-Day Channel and Compute Its Fisher Transform

```
        for(i = 0; i < nLength; ++i) {
    MaxH = Math.max(MaxH, aPrice[i]);
            MinL = Math.min(MinL, aPrice[i]);
}

    Value1 = .5 * 2 * ((vPrice - MinL) /
    (MaxH - MinL) - .5) + .5 * Value1_1;

    if(Value1 > .9999) Value1 = .9999;
    if(Value1 < -.9999) Value1 = -.9999;

    Fish = 0.25 * Math.log((1 + Value1) /
    (1 - Value1)) + .5 * Fish_1;

    return new Array(Fish, Fish_1);
}
```

FIGURE 1.8   *(Continued)*

The Fisher transform of the prices within an eight-day channel is plotted below the price bars in Figure 1.9. Note that the turning points are not only sharp and distinct, but they also occur in a timely fashion so that profitable trades can be entered. The Fisher transform is also compared to a similarly scaled moving average convergence-divergence (MACD) indicator in Figure 1.9. The MACD is representative of conventional indicators whose turning points are rounded and indistinct in comparison to the Fisher transform. As a result of the rounded turning points, the entry and exit signals are invariably late.

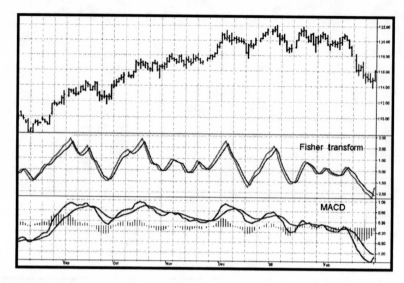

FIGURE 1.9   The Fisher Transform of Normalized Prices Has Very Sharp Turning Points When Compared to Conventional Indicators such as the MACD

KEY POINTS TO REMEMBER

- Prices almost never have a Gaussian, or Normal, probability distribution.
- Statistical measures based on Gaussian probability distributions, such as standard deviations, are in error because the probability distribution assumption underlying the calculation is in error.
- The Fisher transform converts almost any input probability distribution to be nearly a Gaussian probability distribution.
- The Fisher transform, when applied to indicators, provides razor-sharp buy and sell signals.

CHAPTER 2

Trends and Cycles

"That took the wind out of my sails," said Tom disgustedly.

To a trader, Trend Modes and Cycle Modes are synonymous with selection of a trading strategy. In an uptrend the obvious strategy is to buy and hold. Similarly, in a downtrend the strategy is to sell and hold. Conversely, the best strategy in a Cycle Mode is to top-pick and bottom-fish. Traders usually use some variant of moving averages to trade the Trend Mode and some oscillator to trade the Cycle Mode. In either case, the lag induced by the calculations is one of the biggest problems for a trader.

To an analyst, Trend Modes and Cycle Modes are best described by their frequency content. Prices in Trend Modes vary slowly with respect to time. Therefore, Trend Modes disregard high-frequency components and use only the slowly varying low-frequency components. Moving averages are low-pass filters that allow only the low-frequency components to pass to their output, and that is why they are effective for Trend Mode trading. Oscillators are high-pass filters that almost completely disregard the low-frequency components.

I will use these concepts to create a complementary oscillator and moving average. Most important, both the oscillator and the moving average have essentially no lag. The elimination of lag is crucial to the trading indicators and systems developed from them in later chapters. I consider the creation of these zero-lag tools one of the most important developments described in this book. Searching for zero-lag tools has long been the focus of my research, and I have used descriptors such as *Instantaneous Trendline* in previous publications. The techniques I show you in this chapter are entirely new, even if the names are similar.

I will start with the well-known exponential moving average (EMA) to derive an optimum mathematical description of Trend Mode and Cycle Mode components. The equation for an EMA is

$$\text{Output} = \alpha * \text{Input} + (1 - \alpha) * \text{Output}[1] \qquad (2.1)$$

Where α is a number less than 1 and greater than 0

In words, this equation means we take a fraction of the current price and add to it the filtered output one bar ago multiplied by the quantity $(1 - \alpha)$. With these coefficients, if the input is unchanging (zero frequency), the output will eventually converge to the input value. That is, this filter has unity gain at zero frequency. We can describe this filter in terms of its transfer response, which is the output divided by its input. By using Z transform notation, we let Z^{-1} denote one bar of lag as a multiplicative operator. Doing this, the transfer response of Equation 2.1 can be solved using algebra as

$$H(z) = \frac{\text{Output}}{\text{Input}} = \frac{\alpha}{1 - (1 - \alpha) * Z^{-1}} \qquad (2.2)$$

We can test Equation 2.2 by letting Z^{-1} equal +1 (zero frequency). When we do this, it is easy to see that the numerator is equal to the denominator, and so the gain is unity. The high-frequency attenuation of this filter can be tested at the highest possible frequency, the Nyquist frequency, by letting Z^{-1} equal −1. Using daily samples, the highest frequency we can analyze is 0.5 cycles per day (a two-bar cycle). This is the Nyquist frequency for daily data. The two-bar cycle attenuation is $[\alpha/(2 - \alpha)]$. The general attenuation response of the EMA as a function of the frequency is shown in Figure 2.1. The period of a cycle component in Figure 2.1 can be calculated as the reciprocal of frequency. For example, a frequency of 0.1 cycles per day corresponds to a 10-bar period for that cycle component.

In principle, all we have to do to create a high-pass filter is subtract the transfer response of the low-pass filter from unity. The logic is that a transfer response of 1 represents all frequencies, and subtracting the low-pass response from it leaves the high-pass response as a residual. However, there is one problem with this approach: The high-frequency attenuation of the low-pass filter of Equation 2.2 is not infinite (i.e., the transfer response is 0) at the Nyquist frequency. A finite high-frequency response in the low-pass filter will lead to a gain error in the transfer response of the high-pass filter. The finite attenuation problem is eliminated by averaging two sequential input samples rather than using only a single input sample. In this case, the transfer response of the averaged-input low-pass filter is

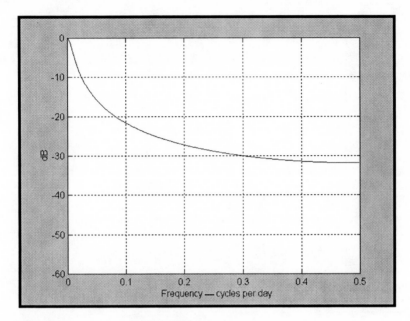

FIGURE 2.1 EMA Frequency Response ($\alpha = 0.05$)

$$H(z) = \frac{\frac{\alpha}{2} * (1 + Z^{-1})}{1 - (1 - \alpha) * Z^{-1}} \qquad (2.3)$$

Equation 2.3 guarantees that the transfer response of the low-pass filter will be 0 when $Z^{-1} = -1$. The general frequency response of the averaged-input EMA is shown in Figure 2.2.

The lag of a simple moving average is approximately half the average length. For example, a 21-bar moving average has a lag of 10 bars. The alpha of an equivalent EMA is related to the length of a simple moving average as

$$\alpha = \frac{2}{\text{Length} + 1} \qquad (2.4)$$

Using Equation 2.4, an EMA using $\alpha = 0.05$ is equivalent to a 39-bar simple moving average. A 39-day simple moving average has a 19-day lag, approximately half its length. Examination of Figure 2.3 shows that the very low-frequency lag of an EMA whose $\alpha = 0.05$ is indeed 19 days. Although the lag decreases as frequency is increased, it is of little consequence because

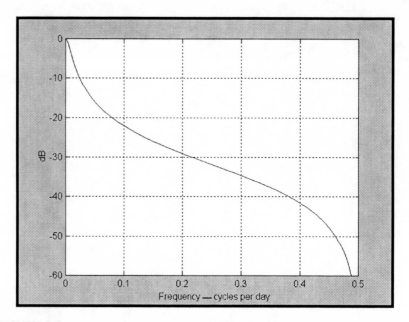

FIGURE 2.2   Smoothed-Input EMA Frequency Response ($\alpha = 0.05$)

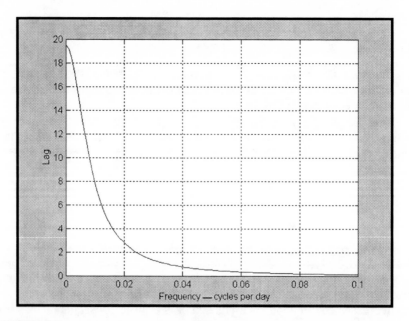

FIGURE 2.3   Smoothed-Input Lag Response ($\alpha = 0.05$)

the filtered amplitude is so small at these frequencies. The real impact of lag of all moving averages is the value of the lag at very low frequencies.

With Equation 2.3 we now have the capacity to construct a high-pass filter. We will subtract Equation 2.3 from unity as

$$HP(z) = 1 - \frac{\frac{\alpha}{2} * (1 + Z^{-1})}{1 - (1 - \alpha) * Z^{-1}}$$

$$= \frac{1 - (1 - \alpha) * Z^{-1} - \frac{\alpha}{2} * (1 + Z^{-1})}{1 - (1 - \alpha) * Z^{-1}}$$

$$= \frac{\left(1 - \frac{\alpha}{2}\right) * (1 - Z^{-1})}{1 - (1 - \alpha) * Z^{-1}}$$

(2.5)

Sharper attenuation can be obtained by using higher-order filters. However, I have learned that higher-order filters not only have greater lag, but they also have transient effects that impress false artifacts on their outputs. This is somewhat like ringing a bell: The ringing is more a function of the bell itself rather than a filtered response of a driving force. A reasonable compromise is the use of a second-order Gaussian filter. A second-order Gaussian low-pass filter can be generated by taking an EMA and immediately taking another identical EMA of the first EMA. This can be represented by squaring the transfer response. We can therefore obtain a second-order Gaussian high-pass filter response by squaring Equation 2.5 as

$$HP(z) = \frac{\left(1 - \frac{\alpha}{2}\right)^2 * (1 - 2 * Z^{-1} + Z^{-2})}{1 - 2 * (1 - \alpha) * Z^{-1} + (1 - \alpha)^2 * Z^{-2}}$$

(2.6)

Equation 2.6 is converted to an EasyLanguage statement as

$$HPF = (1 - \alpha/2)^2 * (Price - 2 * Price[1] + Price[2])$$
$$+ 2 * (1 - \alpha) * HPF[1] - (1 - \alpha)^2 * HPF[2];$$

(2.7)

The transfer responses of Equations 2.6 and 2.7 (they are the same) are plotted in Figure 2.4.

Figure 2.4 shows that only frequency periods longer than 40 bars (frequency = 0.025 cycles per day) are significantly attenuated. Thus we have created a high-pass filter with a relatively sharp cutoff response. Since the output of this filter contains essentially no trending components, it must be the cycle component of price.

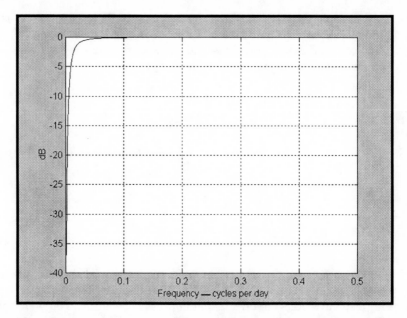

FIGURE 2.4   Transfer Response of a Second-Order High-Pass Gaussian Filter ($\alpha = 0.05$)

The complementary low-pass filter that produces the Instantaneous Trendline is found by subtracting the high-pass components of Equation 2.6 from unity. Skipping over the tedious algebra to put both elements of this subtraction over a common denominator, the equation for the low-pass Instantaneous Trendline is

$$IT(z) = \frac{\left(\alpha - \dfrac{\alpha^2}{4}\right) + \dfrac{\alpha^2}{2}Z^{-1} - \left(\alpha - \dfrac{3\alpha^2}{4}\right)Z^{-2}}{1 - 2 * (1 - \alpha) * Z^{-1} + (1 - \alpha)^2 Z^{-2}} \tag{2.8}$$

Equation 2.8 is converted to an EasyLanguage statement as

$$\begin{aligned}
\text{InstTrend} = &(\alpha - (\alpha/2)^2) * \text{Price} + (\alpha^2/2) * \text{Price}[1] \\
&- (\alpha - 3\alpha^2/4) * \text{Price}[2]) + 2 * (1 - \alpha) \\
&* \text{InstTrend}[1] - (1 - \alpha)^2 * \text{InstTrend}[2]; \tag{2.9}
\end{aligned}$$

Figure 2.5 shows the attenuation of the Instantaneous Trendline filter and how only the low-frequency components are passed. The attenuation characteristic of the Instantaneous Trendline in Figure 2.5 is almost identical to that of the EMA shown in Figure 2.2.

The most important feature of the Instantaneous Trendline is that it

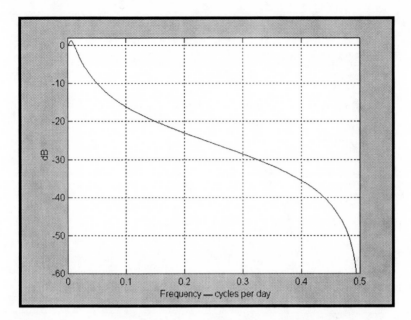

FIGURE 2.5 Frequency Response of the Instantaneous Trendline Filter ($\alpha = 0.05$)

has zero lag. That's right—*zero lag!* The lag is 0 because Instantaneous Trendline was created by subtracting the transfer response of a high-pass filter from unity. Since the high-pass filter has a very small amplitude at low frequencies, the resulting low-frequency lag of the difference is just the lag of unity, which is 0. Figure 2.6 shows the lag profile of the Instantaneous Trendline as a function of frequency. While the lag does increase to 13 bars at an approximate frequency of 0.005 cycles per day (200-day period), a frequency that low is more important to investors than to traders.

The importance of the zero lag feature of the Instantaneous Trendline is demonstrated by comparing its response to an EMA having an equivalent alpha. Figure 2.7 gives this comparison in response to real market data. It is clear that the two averages have about the same degree of smoothing, but that the Instantaneous Trendline has zero lag. If it is more convenient, you can think of the Instantaneous Trendline as a centered moving average. The major advantage of the Instantaneous Trendline compared to the centered moving average is that it can be used up to the right edge of the chart. That means that real indicators and trading systems can be built using it as a component. It is also clear that the lag of the Instantaneous Trendline is so small that a trader can begin to think about creating indicators and trading systems as a function of the price crisscrossing it. In later chapters we will develop such indicators and trading systems.

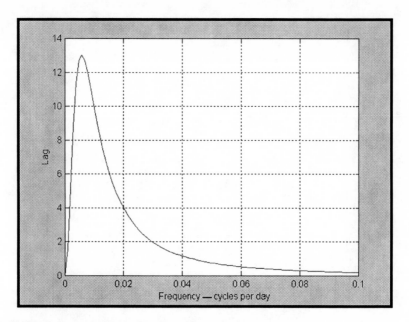

FIGURE 2.6   Lag of the Instantaneous Trendline Filter ($\alpha = 0.05$)

FIGURE 2.7   Instantaneous Trendline Has Much Less Lag than an EMA ($\alpha = 0.05$)

KEY POINTS TO REMEMBER

- The Instantaneous Trendline has zero lag.
- The Instantaneous Trendline has about the same smoothing as an EMA using the same alpha.
- An EMA is a low-pass filter.
- Higher-order Gaussian filters are the equivalent of applying the EMA multiple times.
- Using filters higher than second order is not advisable because of the ringing transient responses of the higher-order filters.
- A complementary cycle oscillator to the Instantaneous Trendline exists as a second-order high-pass filter.
- The lag of the complementary cycle oscillator is 0.

CHAPTER 3

Trading
the Trend

"The market is going up," said Tom trendedly.

Having an Instantaneous Trendline with zero lag (Equations 2.8 and 2.9) is a good beginning to generate a responsive trend-following system. The system would be even more responsive if it contained a trigger that preceded the Instantaneous Trendline rather than following it and offering a confirming signal. A leading trigger can be generated by adding a two-day momentum of the Instantaneous Trendline to the Instantaneous Trendline itself.

The rationale for the leading trigger is that adding the two-day momentum to the current value in a trend is predicting where the Instantaneous Trendline will be two days from now. When plotting the trigger on the current bar, the trigger must lead the Instantaneous Trendline by two bars. On a more mathematical level, the lag of the trigger is shown in Figure 3.1. The figure shows that the low-frequency lead is two bars and the worst-case lag occurs at a frequency of 0.25 cycles per day (a four-bar cycle period). The lag is of no concern because the attenuation of the Instantaneous Trendline (shown in Figure 2.5) makes the amplitude of the components in the vicinity of 0.25 cycles per day almost irrelevant to the overall response.

There is a price to pay for achieving the lead response of the trigger. That price is that leading functions cause a higher-frequency gain in the filter instead of attenuation, which has a smoothing effect. Therefore, high-frequency gain causes the resulting transfer response to look more ragged than the original function. This is the case for any momentum function. The gain response of the trigger has a maximum of 9.5 dB at a frequency of 0.25 cycles per day, as shown in Figure 3.2. In this case, the gain does not

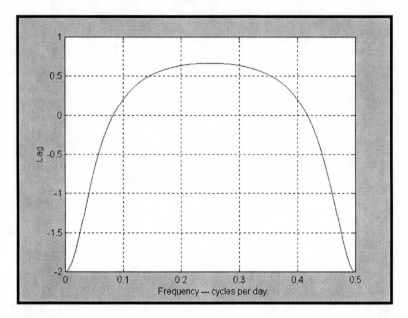

FIGURE 3.1   Lead and Lag of the Trigger as a Function of Frequency

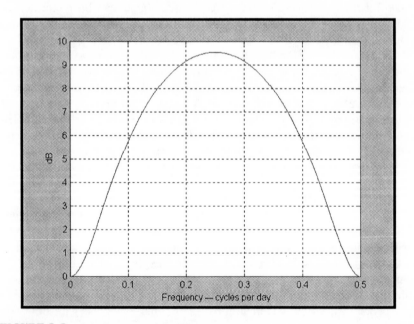

FIGURE 3.2   Gain Response of the Trigger

severely affect the smoothness of the trigger because the Instantaneous Trendline has an attenuation of 26 dB at 0.25 cycles per day, as shown in Figure 2.5. Therefore, using both terms to compute the net attenuation, the worst-case high-frequency smoothing attenuation is still about 16 dB. This means the trigger will have about the same degree of smoothness as the Instantaneous Trendline.

The Instantaneous Trendline and the Trigger of the trend-following system are shown as indicators in Figure 3.3; the EasyLanguage code to create these indicator lines is shown in Figure 3.4, and the eSignal Formula Script (EFS) code is shown in Figure 3.5. The process for creating a trend-following trading system from the indicators is simple. One unique aspect of the code is that the ITrend is forced to be a finite impulse response (FIR)-smoothed version of price for the first seven bars of the calculation. This initialization is included to cause the ITrend to converge more rapidly to its correct value from the beginning transient. The strategy enters a long position when the trigger crosses over the Instantaneous Trendline and enters a short position when the trigger crosses under the Instantaneous Trendline. However, an effective trading system is more than following a simple set of indicators.

First, experience has shown that greater profits result from using limit orders rather than market orders or stop orders. Market orders are self-explanatory. Stop orders mean the market must be going in the direction of the trade before the order is filled. For example, for long-position trades, the stop order must be placed above the current price. Thus, the price must

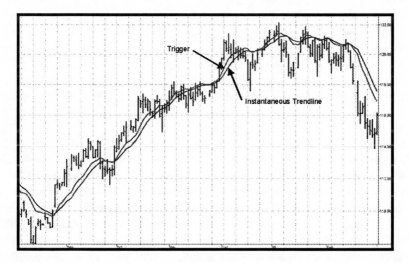

FIGURE 3.3 Crossing of the Trigger and Instantaneous Trendline are Trading Signals

```
Inputs:              Price((H+L)/2),
                     alpha(.07);

Vars:                Smooth(0),
                     ITrend(0),
                     Trigger(0);

ITrend = (alpha - alpha*alpha/4)*Price
    + .5*alpha*alpha*Price[1] - (alpha
    - .75*alpha*alpha)*Price[2] + 2
    *(1 - alpha)*ITrend[1] - (1 - alpha)
    *(1 - alpha)*Itrend[2];
If currentbar < 7 then ITrend = (Price + 2*Price[1]
    + Price[2]) / 4;
Trigger = 2*Itrend - ITrend[2];

Plot1(Itrend, "ITrend");
Plot2(Trigger, "Trig");
```

FIGURE 3.4 EasyLanguage Code for the ITrend Indicator

increase from its current level before you get stopped into the long-position trade. This means you necessarily give up some of the profits you would otherwise have gotten if you had entered on a market order at the instant of your signal. You can lose additional profits from stop orders due to slippage. Slippage is the difference between your stop value and the price at which your order actually got filled. In fast markets slippage can be substantial. If limit orders are placed for the long position, the limit price must be below the current price. That is, the market must move against your anticipated trade before you get a fill. This means that if the price drops sufficiently so that your limit order is filled, you have captured additional profits if the price subsequently reverses and goes in the direction of your signal. Furthermore, if there is any slippage in filling the limit order, the slippage will be negative because it is going in the direction opposite to your intended trade. When the price turns around and goes in the direction of your signals, you have therefore captured the slippage as profit. In the EasyLanguage trading strategy code of Figure 3.6, I have set the level of the limit order to be 35 percent of the current bar's range added onto the closing price of the current bar (in the case of a short signal) or subtracted from the closing price of the current bar (in the case of a long signal). The 35 percent is the input variable RngFrac, and is an optimizable parameter.

```
/*********************************************************
Title:               Instantaneous Trendline
*****************************************************/

function preMain() {
    setPriceStudy(true);
    setStudyTitle("Instantaneous Trendline");
    setCursorLabelName("IT", 0);
    setDefaultBarThickness(2, 0);
}

var a = 0.05;
var IT = 0;
var IT1 = 0;
var IT2 = 0;
var Price = 0;
var Price1 = 0;
var Price2 = 0;

function main() {
    if (getBarState() == BARSTATE_NEWBAR) {
        IT2 = IT1;
        IT1 = IT;
        Price2 = Price1;
        Price1 = Price;
    }

    Price = close();

    IT = (a-((a/2)*(a/2)))*Price + ((a*a)/2)*Price1
       - (a-(3*(a*a))/4)*Price2 + 2*(1-a)*IT1
       - ((1-a)*(1-a))*IT2;

        return (IT);
}
```

FIGURE 3.5 EFS Code for the ITrend Indicator

Unfortunately, not all trading signals are perfect. In fact, with the crossover strategy that I have developed it is possible to be on the wrong side of the trade for a substantial period from time to time. For this reason, I have added a rule that if the price goes against your position by more than some percentage, the strategy will correct itself and automatically reverse to the opposite position. The percentage is supplied as the input variable

```
Inputs:                 Price((H+L)/2),
                        alpha(.07),
                        RngFrac(.35),
                        RevPct(1.015);

Vars:                   Smooth(0),
                        ITrend(0),
                        Trigger(0);

ITrend = (alpha - alpha*alpha/4)*Price
    + .5*alpha*alpha*Price[1] - (alpha
    - .75*alpha*alpha)*Price[2] + 2
    *(1 - alpha)*ITrend[1] - (1 - alpha)
    *(1 - alpha)*ITrend[2];
If currentbar < 7 then ITrend = (Price + 2*Price[1]
    + Price[2]) / 4;
Trigger = 2*Itrend - ITrend[2];

If Trigger Crosses Over ITrend then Buy Next Bar at
    Close - RngFrac*(High - Low) Limit;
If Trigger Crosses Under ITrend then Sell Short Next
    Bar at Close + RngFrac*(High - Low) Limit;

If MarketPosition = 1 and Close < EntryPrice/RevPct
    then Sell Short Next Bar On Open;
If MarketPosition = -1 and Close > RevPct*EntryPrice
    then Buy Next Bar on Open;
```

FIGURE 3.6   EasyLanguage Code for the Instantaneous Trendline Trading Strategy

RevPct. RevPct is an optimizable parameter, but I find that the default value of 1.5 percent (RevPct = 1.015) is a relatively robust number. The same strategy for EFS code is given in Figure 3.7.

I applied the strategy code of Figures 3.6 and 3.7 to several currency futures because it is well known that currencies tend to trend. I additionally introduced a $2,500 money management stop to further avoid giving back accumulated profits. Doing this, I achieved the trading results shown in Table 3.1. The time span is on the order of a quarter century, and a relatively large number of trades are taken. The Instantaneous Trend Strategy consists of only a few independent parameters. Since the ratio of the number of trades to the number of parameters is large and since the trading took place over a large time span, it is highly unlikely that the strategy has

```
/*********************************************************
Title:          ITrend Trading Strategy
Coded By:   Chris D. Kryza (Divergence Software, Inc.)
Email:      c.kryza@gte.net
Incept:    06/27/2003
Version:   1.0.0



=========================================================
Fix History:

06/27/2003 -    Initial Release
1.0.0


=========================================================
*********************************************************/


//External Variables

var grID                     = 0;
var nBarCount                = 0;
var xOver                    = 0;
var nStatus                  = 0;
var nEntryPrice              = 0;
var nDirection               = 0;
var nLimitPrice              = 0;
var nAdj1                    = null;

var aPriceArray              = new Array();
var aITrendArray             = new Array();


//== PreMain function required by eSignal to set_
   things up
function preMain() {
var x;

    setPriceStudy(true);
    setStudyTitle("ITrend Strategy");
    setCursorLabelName("ITrend", 0);
    setCursorLabelName("Trig", 1);

                                        (continued)
```

FIGURE 3.7   EFS Code for the Instantaneous Trendline Trading Strategy

```
    setDefaultBarFgColor( Color.blue, 0 );
    setDefaultBarFgColor( Color.red,  1 );

      //initialize arrays
    for (x=0; x<10; x++) {
      aPriceArray[x]              = 0.0;
      aITrendArray[x]             = 0.0;
    }

}

//== Main processing function
function main( Alpha, RngFrac, RevPct ) {
var x;
var nPrice;

    if (getCurrentBarIndex() == 0) return;

        //initialize parameters if necessary
        if ( Alpha == null ) {
                Alpha = 0.07;
        }
        if ( RngFrac == null ) {
                RngFrac = 0.35;
        }
        if ( RevPct == null ) {
                RevPct = 1.015;
        }

        // study is initializing
    if (getBarState() == BARSTATE_ALLBARS) {
      return null;
    }

    if (nAdj1 == null) nAdj1 = (high()-low()) * 0.20;

        //on each new bar, save array values
        if ( getBarState() == BARSTATE_NEWBAR ) {

                nBarCount++;

                aPriceArray.pop();
                aPriceArray.unshift( 0 );
```

FIGURE 3.7 (Continued)

```
            aITrendArray.pop();
            aITrendArray.unshift( 0 );

      }

      nPrice = ( high()+low() ) / 2;
      aPriceArray[0] = nPrice;

      if (aPriceArray[2] == 0) return;

      if ( nBarCount < 7 ) {
            aITrendArray[0] = (nPrice
                + 2*aPriceArray[1]
                + aPriceArray[2])/4;
      }
      else {
            aITrendArray[0] = (Alpha
                - Alpha*Alpha/4)*nPrice
                + 0.5*Alpha*Alpha*aPriceArray[1]
                - (Alpha - 0.75*Alpha*Alpha)
                * aPriceArray[2] + 2*(1-Alpha)
                *aITrendArray[1] - (1-Alpha)
                *(1-Alpha)*aITrendArray[2];
      }

      if (aITrendArray[2] == 0) return;

      nTrig = 2 * aITrendArray[0] - aITrendArray[2];

      nStatus = 0;
      if ( Strategy.isLong() )  nStatus =  1;
      if ( Strategy.isShort() ) nStatus = -1;

 var bReverseTrade = false;
      if ( nStatus == 1 && close()
          < (nEntryPrice/RevPct) ) {
            ReverseToShort();
            bReverseTrade = true;
      } else if ( nStatus == -1 && close()
          > (RevPct*nEntryPrice) ) {
            ReverseToLong();
            bReverseTrade = true;
                                      (continued)
```

FIGURE 3.7   *(Continued)*

```
        }
        //check for new signals
if (bReverseTrade == false) {
   if ( nTrig > aITrendArray[0] ) {
      if ( xOver == -1 && nStatus != 1) {
         nLimitPrice = Math.max(low(), (close()
            - ( high()-low() )*RngFrac));
         LongLimit( nLimitPrice );
         nDirection = 1;
      }
      xOver = 1;
   } else if ( nTrig < aITrendArray[0]  ) {
      if ( xOver == 1 && nStatus != -1) {
         nLimitPrice = Math.min(high(), (close()
            + ( high()-low() )*RngFrac));
         ShortLimit( nLimitPrice );
         nDirection = -1;
      }
      xOver = -1;
   }
        }

        if (!isNaN( aITrendArray[0] ) ) {
                return new Array( aITrendArray[0],_
                nTrig );
        }
}


function LongLimit( nPrice ) {
        Strategy.doLong("Long", Strategy.LIMIT,_
           Strategy.THISBAR, Strategy.DEFAULT,_
           nPrice );
        nEntryPrice = nPrice;
   drawShapeRelative(0, low()-nAdj1, Shape.UPARROW,_
      "", Color.lime, Shape.ONTOP, gID());
        return;
}

function ShortLimit( nPrice ) {
        Strategy.doShort("Short", Strategy.LIMIT,_
           Strategy.THISBAR, Strategy.DEFAULT,_
           nPrice );
```

FIGURE 3.7   *(Continued)*

```
            nEntryPrice = nPrice;
            debugPrintln(getCurrentBarIndex()
                + " short  " + nPrice);
     drawShapeRelative(0, high()+nAdj1,Shape.DOWNARROW,_
        "", Color.maroon, Shape.ONTOP, gID());
            return;
}

function ReverseToLong() {
        Strategy.doLong("Reverse to Long",_
            Strategy.MARKET, Strategy.NEXTBAR,_
            Strategy.DEFAULT );
        DrawShapeRelative(1, low(1)-nAdj1,_
            Shape.UPARROW, "", Color.lime,_
            Shape.ONTOP, gID());
        nEntryPrice = open(1);
        nStatus     = 1;
        nDirection  = 0;
        nLimitPrice = 0;
        return;
}

function ReverseToShort() {
        Strategy.doShort("Reverse to Short",_
            Strategy.MARKET, Strategy.NEXTBAR,_
            Strategy.DEFAULT );
        drawShapeRelative(1, high(1)+nAdj1,_
            Shape.DOWNARROW, "", Color.maroon,_
            Shape.ONTOP, gID());
        nEntryPrice = open(1);
        nStatus     = -1;
        nDirection  = 0;
        nLimitPrice = 0;
        return;
}

//== gID function assigns unique identifier to_
    graphic/text routines
function gID() {
    grID ++;
    return( grID );
}
```

FIGURE 3.7 *(Continued)*

TABLE 3.1 Sample Trading Results Using the Instantaneous
Trendline Strategy

Future	Net Profit	Number of Trades	Percent Profitable	Profit Factor	Max DD
EC (4/81–3/03)	$201,812	230	42.2%	1.89	($26,775)
JY (9/81–3/03)	$221,312	229	48.5%	2.50	($11,712)
SF (6/76–3/03)	$129,175	337	45.1%	1.52	($15,387)

been curve fitted. Curve fitting is a weakness of many technical analysis
trading strategies.

Please allow me to brag about the Instantaneous Trendline Strategy.
(Perhaps it is not bragging, because as Muhammed Ali said, "It ain't bragging if you can really do it.") The performance results of this strategy are
comparable to, or exceed, the performance of commercial systems costing
thousands of dollars. You can create synthetic equity growth curves using
the established percentage of profitable trades and profit factors. This is
explained in Chapter 15. You will find the equity growth trading the currencies in Table 3.1 to be remarkably consistent.

KEY POINTS TO REMEMBER

- The Instantaneous Trendline has zero lag.
- The Instantaneous Trendline has about the same smoothing as an
  exponential moving average (EMA) using the same alpha.
- The smoothing enables the use of a trading trigger that has a two-bar
  lead.
- Trading signals are generated by the crossing of the Trigger line and the
  Instantaneous Trendline.
- Trade entries are made on limit orders to capture a larger range of the
  trade and to eliminate slippage losses.
- Major losses are avoided by recognizing when a trade is on the wrong
  side and reversing position.
- The Instantaneous Trendline Strategy can be optimized for application
  to many stocks and commodity markets.

CHAPTER 4

Trading
the Cycle

"It happens again and again," said Tom periodically.

E quation 2.5 described a high-pass filter that isolated the cycle mode components. Essentially all that need be done to generate a cycle-based indicator is to plot the results of this equation. However, some smoothing is required to remove the two-bar and three-bar components that detract from the interpretation of the cyclic signals. These components can be removed with a simple finite impulse response (FIR)[1] low-pass filter as

$$\text{Smooth} = (\text{Price} + 2 * \text{Price}[1] + 2 * \text{Price}[2] + \text{Price}[3])/6; \quad (4.1)$$

The lag of the Smooth filter of Equation 4.1 is 1.5 bars at all frequencies. Figure 4.1 demonstrates that the Smooth filter eliminates the two- and three-bar cycle components. The Smooth filter is to be used as an additional filter to remove the distracting very-high-frequency components, thus creating an indicator that is easier to interpret for trading.

The EasyLanguage code to make a cycle component indicator is given in Figure 4.2 and the eSignal Formula Script (EFS) code is given in Figure 4.3. I call this the Cyber Cycle Indicator. After the inputs and variables are defined, the smoothing filter of Equation 4.1 and the high-pass filter of Equation 2.7 are computed. They are followed by an initialization condition that facilitates a rapid convergence at the beginning of the input data. A trading trigger signal is created by delaying the cycle by one bar.

Trading the Cyber Cycle Indicator is straightforward. Buy when the Cycle line crosses over the Trigger line. You are at the bottom of the cycle

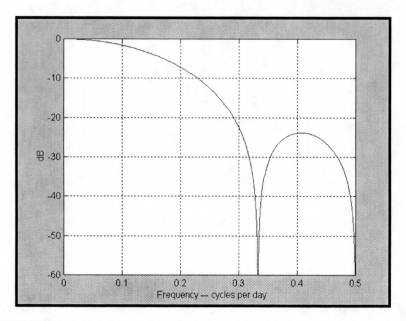

FIGURE 4.1 A Four-Element FIR Filter Eliminates Two- and Three-Bar Cycles

```
Inputs:              Price((H+L)/2),
                     alpha(.07);

Vars:                Smooth(0),
                     Cycle(0);

Smooth = (Price + 2*Price[1] + 2*Price[2]
   + Price[3])/6;
Cycle = (1 - .5*alpha)*(1 - .5*alpha)*(Smooth
   - 2*Smooth[1] + Smooth[2]) + 2*(1 - alpha)
   *Cycle[1] - (1 - alpha)*(1 - alpha)*Cycle[2];
If currentbar < 7 then Cycle = (Price - 2*Price[1]
   + Price[2]) / 4;

Plot1(Cycle, "Cycle");
Plot2(Cycle[1], "Trigger");
```

FIGURE 4.2 EasyLanguage Code for the Cyber Cycle Indicator

```
/*********************************************************
Title:              Cyber Cycle
*********************************************************/

function preMain() {
    setStudyTitle("High Pass Filter");
    setCursorLabelName("HPF",0);
    setDefaultBarThickness(2, 0);
}

var a = 0.07;
var HPF = 0;
var HPF1 = 0;
var HPF2 = 0;
var Price = 0;
var Price1 = 0;
var Price2 = 0;

function main() {
    if (getBarState() == BARSTATE_NEWBAR) {
        HPF2 = HPF1;
        HPF1 = HPF;
        Price2 = Price1;
        Price1 = Price;
    }

    Price = close();

    HPF = ((1-(a/2))*(1-(a/2))) * (Price - 2*Price1
        + Price2) + 2*(1-a)*HPF1 - ((1-a)*(1-a))*HPF2;

        return (HPF);
}
```

FIGURE 4.3   EFS Code for the Cyber Cycle Indicator

at this point. Sell when the Cycle line crosses under the Trigger line. You are at the top of the cycle in this case. Figure 4.4 illustrates that each of the major turning points is captured by the Cycle line crossing the Trigger line. To be sure, there are crossings at other than the cyclic turning points. Many of these can be eliminated by discretionary traders using their experience or others of their favorite tools.

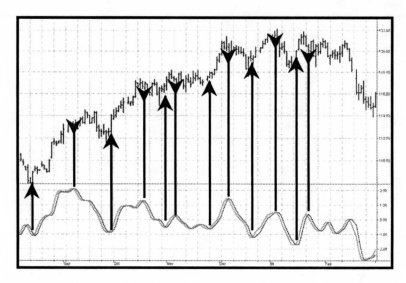

FIGURE 4.4   The Cyber Cycle Indicator Catches Every Significant Turning Point

One of the more interesting aspects of the Cyber Cycle is that it was developed simultaneously with the Instantaneous Trendline. They are opposite sides of the same coin because the total frequency content of the market being analyzed is in one indicator or the other. This is important because the conventional methods of using moving averages and oscillators can be dispensed with. The significance of this duality is demonstrated in Figure 4.5.

A low-lag four-bar weighted moving average (WMA) is plotted in Figure 4.5 for comparison with the action of the Instantaneous Trendline. Note that each time the WMA crosses the Instantaneous Trendline the Cyber Cycle Oscillator is also crossing its zero line. Since there is essentially no lag in the Instantaneous Trendline we can, for the first time, use an indicator overlay on prices in exactly the same way we have traditionally used oscillators. That is, when the prices cross the Instantaneous Trendline you can start to prepare for a reversal when prices reach a maximum excursion from the Instantaneous Trendline. Since there is only a small lag in the Instantaneous Trendline, it represents a short-term mean of prices. This being the case, we can use the old principle that prices revert to their mean.

But what is the best way to exploit the mean reversion? The false signals arising from use of the Cyber Cycle are more problematic for automatic trading systems. The first thing that must be understood about indicators is that they are invariably late. No indicator can precede an event from which it is derived. This is particularly important when trading short-term cycles.

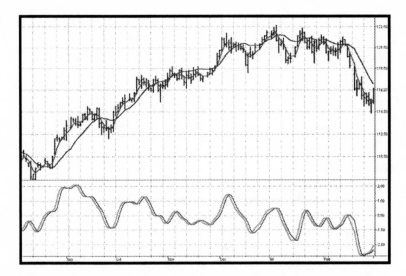

FIGURE 4.5 The Instantaneous Trendline and Cyber Cycle Oscillator are Duals

We need an indicator that predicts the turning point so the trade can be made at the turning point or even before it occurs. In the code of Figure 4.2 we know we induce 1.5 bars of lag due to the calculation of Smooth. The cycle equation contributes some small amount of lag also, perhaps half a bar. The Trigger lags the Cycle by one bar, so that their crossing introduces at least another bar of lag. Finally, we can't execute the trade until the bar after the signal is observed. In total, that means our trade execution will be at least four bars late. If we are working with an eight-bar cycle, that means the signal will be exactly wrong. We could do better to buy when the signal says sell, and vice versa.

The difficulties arising from the lag suggest a way to build an automatic trading strategy. Suppose we choose to use the trading signal in the opposite direction of the signal. That will work if we can introduce lag so the correct signal will be given in the more general case, not just the case of an eight-bar cycle. Figure 4.6 is the EasyLanguage code for the Cyber Cycle strategy. It starts exactly the same as the Cyber Cycle Indicator. I then introduce the variable Signal, which is an exponential moving average of the Cycle variable. The exponential moving average generates the desired lag in the trading signal. As derived in *Rocket Science for Traders*,[2] the relationship between the alpha of an exponential moving average and lag is

$$\alpha = \frac{1}{\text{Lag} + 1} \tag{4.2}$$

```
Inputs:          Price((H+L)/2),
                 alpha(.07),
                 Lag(9);

Vars:            Smooth(0),
                 Cycle(0),
                 alpha2(0),
                 Signal(0);

Smooth = (Price + 2*Price[1] + 2*Price[2]
    + Price[3])/6;
Cycle = (1 - .5*alpha)*(1 - .5*alpha)*(Smooth
    - 2*Smooth[1] + Smooth[2]) + 2*(1 - alpha)
    *Cycle[1] - (1 - alpha)*(1 - alpha)*Cycle[2];
If currentbar < 7 then Cycle = (Price - 2*Price[1]
    + Price[2]) / 4;

alpha2 = 1 / (Lag + 1);
Signal = alpha2*Cycle + (1 - alpha2)*Signal[1];

If Signal Crosses Under Signal[1] then Buy Next_
    Bar on Open;
If Signal Crosses Over Signal[1] then Sell Short Next_
    Bar on Open;

If MarketPosition = 1 and PositionProfit
    < 0 and BarsSinceEntry > 8 then Sell This Bar;
If MarketPosition = -1 and PositionProfit
    < 0 and BarsSinceEntry > 8 then Buy To Cover This Bar;
```

FIGURE 4.6 EasyLanguage Code for the Cyber Cycle Trading Strategy

This relationship is used to create the variable alpha2 in the code and the variable Signal using the exponential moving average.

The trading signals using the variable Signal crossing itself delayed by one bar are exactly the opposite of the trading signals I would have used if there were no delay. But, since the variable Signal is delayed such that the net delay is less than half a cycle, the trading signals are correct to catch the next cyclic reversal.

The idea of betting against the correct direction by waiting for the next cycle reversal can be pretty scary because that reversal may "never" happen because the market takes off in a trend. For this reason I included two lines of code that are escape mechanisms if we were wrong in our entry signal. These last two lines of code in Figure 4.6 reverse the trading position if we have been in the trade for more than eight bars and the trade has an open position loss.

The EFS code for the Cyber Cycle Trading Strategy is given in Figure 4.7.

The trading strategy of Figures 4.6 and 4.7 was applied to Treasury Bond futures because this contract tends to cycle and not stay in a trend for long periods. The performance response from January 4, 1988 to March 3, 2003, a period in excess of 15 years, produced the results shown in Table 4.1. These performance results, and the consistent equity growth depicted in Figure 4.8, exceed the results of most commercially available trading systems designed for Treasury Bonds.

```
/*********************************************************
Title:       Cyber Cycle Trading Strategy
Coded By:    Chris D. Kryza (Divergence Software, Inc.)
Email:    c.kryza@gte.net
Incept:   06/27/2003
Version:  1.0.0



=========================================================
Fix History:

06/27/2003 -    Initial Release
1.0.0


=========================================================
*********************************************************/


//External Variables

var grID              = 0;
var nBarCount         = 0;
var nStatus           = 0; //0=flat, -1=short,_
                                1=long
//var nTrigger         = 0; //buy/sell on next open
var nBarsInTrade      = 0;
var nEntryPrice       = 0;
                                    (continued)
```

FIGURE 4.7 EFS Code for the Cyber Cycle Trading Strategy

```
var nAdj1                      = 0;
var nAdj2                      = 0;

var aPriceArray                = new Array();
var aSmoothArray               = new Array();
var aCycleArray                = new Array();
var aSignalArray               = new Array();


//== PreMain function required by eSignal to set_
    things up
function preMain() {
var x;

  //setPriceStudy( true );
  setStudyTitle("CyberCycle Strategy");
      //setShowCursorLabel( false );

      setCursorLabelName("Signal ", 0);
      setCursorLabelName("Signal1", 1);

      setDefaultBarFgColor(Color.blue, 0);
      setDefaultBarFgColor(Color.red, 1);


      //initialize arrays
  for (x=0; x<10; x++) {
      aPriceArray[x]     = 0.0;
      aSmoothArray[x]    = 0.0;
      aCycleArray[x]     = 0.0;
      aSignalArray[x]    = 0.0;
  }

}

//== Main processing function
function main( Alpha, Lag ) {
var x;
var nPrice;
var nAlpha2;
```

FIGURE 4.7   *(Continued)*

```
if (getCurrentBarIndex() == 0) return;

    //initialize parameters if necessary
    if ( Alpha == null ) {
        Alpha = 0.07;
    }

    if ( Lag == null ) {
        Lag = 20;
    }

    // study is initializing
if (getBarState() == BARSTATE_ALLBARS) {
  return null;
}

    //on each new bar, save array values
    if ( getBarState() == BARSTATE_NEWBAR ) {

        nBarCount++;
        nBarsInTrade++;

        //variables for image alignment
        nAdj1 = (high()-low()) * 0.20;
        nAdj2 = (high()-low()) * 0.35;

        aPriceArray.pop();
        aPriceArray.unshift( 0 );

        aSmoothArray.pop();
        aSmoothArray.unshift( 0 );

        aCycleArray.pop();
        aCycleArray.unshift( 0 );

        aSignalArray.pop();
        aSignalArray.unshift( 0 );
}

    //Cyber Cycle formula
    nPrice = ( high()+low() ) / 2;
```

(continued)

FIGURE 4.7   *(Continued)*

```
        aPriceArray[0] = nPrice;

if (aPriceArray[3] == 0) return;

        aSmoothArray[0] = ( aPriceArray[0]
            + 2*aPriceArray[1] + 2*aPriceArray[2]
            + aPriceArray[3] ) / 6;

        if ( nBarCount < 7 ) {
            aCycleArray[0] = ( aPriceArray[0]
                - 2*aPriceArray[1]
                + aPriceArray[2] ) / 4;
        }
        else {
            aCycleArray[0] = ( 1 - 0.5*Alpha )
                * ( 1 - 0.5*Alpha )
                * ( aSmoothArray[0]
                - 2*aSmoothArray[1]
                + aSmoothArray[2] ) + 2*( 1-Alpha )
                * aCycleArray[1] - ( 1-Alpha )
                * ( 1-Alpha ) * aCycleArray[2];
        }


        //create the actual trading signals
        nAlpha2 = 1 / (Lag + 1 );
        aSignalArray[0] = nAlpha2 * aCycleArray[0]
            + ( 1.0 - nAlpha2 ) * aSignalArray[1];


        //process our trading strategy code
        //=================================

        nStatus = 0;
        if (Strategy.isLong() == true) nStatus = 1;
        if (Strategy.isShort() == true) nStatus = -1;

        //currently not in a trade so look for a trigger
        if ( nBarCount > 10 && nStatus == 0 ) {
            //signal cross down - we buy
            if ( aSignalArray[0] < aSignalArray[1]_
```

FIGURE 4.7 (Continued)

```
                    && aSignalArray[1]
                    >= aSignalArray[2] ) {
                        goLong();
                }
                //signal cross up - we sell
                if ( aSignalArray[0] > aSignalArray[1]_
                    && aSignalArray[1]
                    <= aSignalArray[2] ) {
                        goShort();
                }
        }
        //currently in a trade so look for profit stop_
            or reversal
        else if ( nBarCount > 10 && nStatus != 0 ) {
                if ( nStatus == 1 ) { //in a long trade
                        //if trade is unprofitable after_
                            8 bars, exit position
                        if ( close() - nEntryPrice
                            < 0 && nBarsInTrade > 8 ) {
                                closeLong();
                        }
                        //otherwise, check for trigger in_
                            other direction
                        if ( aSignalArray[0]
                            > aSignalArray[1]_
                            && aSignalArray[1]
                            <= aSignalArray[2] ) {
                                goShort();
                        }
                } else if ( nStatus == -1 ) { //in a_
                    short trade
                        //if trade is unprofitable after_
                            8 bars, exit position
                        if ( nEntryPrice - close() < 0_
                            && nBarsInTrade > 8 ) {
                                closeShort();
                        }
                        //otherwise, check for trigger in_
                            other direction
                        if ( aSignalArray[0]
                            < aSignalArray[1]_
                                                    (continued)
```

FIGURE 4.7   *(Continued)*

```
                             && aSignalArray[1]
                             >= aSignalArray[2] ) {
                                 goLong();
                         }
                 }
         }

         return new Array(aSignalArray[0],_
             aSignalArray[1]);
}


//enter a short trade
function goShort() {
         drawShapeRelative(1, aSignalArray[1],_
             Shape.DOWNARROW, "",
             Color.maroon, Shape.ONTOP|Shape.BOTTOM,
             gID());
             Strategy.doShort("Short Signal",_
             Strategy.MARKET, Strategy.NEXTBAR,
             Strategy.DEFAULT );
         nStatus        = -1;
         nEntryPrice    = open(1);
         nBarsInTrade = 1;
}

//exit a short trade
function closeShort() {
         drawShapeRelative(-0, aSignalArray[0],_
             Shape.DIAMOND, "",
             Color.maroon, Shape.ONTOP|Shape.TOP, gID());
         Strategy.doCover("Cover Short",_
             Strategy.MARKET, Strategy.THISBAR,_
             Strategy.ALL );
         nStatus      = 0;
         nEntryPrice  = 0;
}

//enter a long trade
function goLong() {
         drawShapeRelative(1, aSignalArray[1],_
```

FIGURE 4.7   (Continued)

```
          Shape.UPARROW, "",
            Color.lime, Shape.ONTOP|Shape.TOP, gID());
        Strategy.doLong("Long Signal", Strategy.MARKET,_
          Strategy.NEXTBAR, Strategy.DEFAULT );
        nStatus          = 1;
        nEntryPrice      = open(1);
        nBarsInTrade = 1;
}

//exit a long trade
function closeLong() {
  drawShapeRelative(0, aSignalArray[0],_
    Shape.DIAMOND, "",
    Color.lime, Shape.ONTOP|Shape.BOTTOM, gID());
      Strategy.doSell("Sell Long", Strategy.MARKET,_
        Strategy.THISBAR, Strategy.ALL );
      nStatus      = 0;
      nEntryPrice  = 0;
}

//== gID function assigns unique identifier to
    graphic/text routines
function gID() {
    grID ++;
    return( grID );
}
```

FIGURE 4.7   *(Continued)*

TABLE 4.1   Fifteen-Year Performance of the Cyber Cycle Trading System Trading Treasury Bond Futures

Net profit	$93,156
Number of trades	430
Percent profitable	56.7%
Profit factor	1.44
Max drawdown	($12,500)
Profit/trade	$216.64

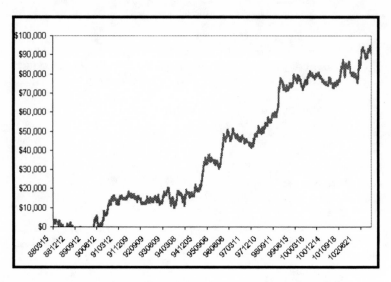

FIGURE 4.8   Cyber Cycle Trading System 15-Year Equity Growth Trading Treasury Bonds

KEY POINTS TO REMEMBER

- All indicators have lag.
- The Instantaneous Trendline and the Cyber Cycle Indicator are complementary. This enables traders to use indicators overlaid on prices the same way conventional oscillators are used.
- A viable cycle-based trading system delays the signal slightly less than a half cycle to generate leading turning point entry and exit signals.
- Major losses are avoided by recognizing when a trade is on the wrong side and reversing position.

CHAPTER 5

The CG Oscillator

"Add up this list of n numbers and then divide the sum by n,"
said Tom meanly.

I n this chapter I describe a new oscillator that is unique because it is smoothed and has essentially zero lag. The smoothing enables clear identification of turning points and the zero-lag aspect enables action to be taken early in the move. This oscillator, which is the serendipitous result of my research into adaptive filters, has substantial advantages over conventional oscillators used in technical analysis. The CG in the name of the oscillator stands for the center of gravity of the prices over the window of observation.

The center of gravity (CG) of a physical object is its balance point. For example, if you balance a 12-inch ruler on your finger, the CG will be at its 6-inch point. If you change the weight distribution of the ruler by putting a paper clip on one end, then the balance point (i.e., the CG) shifts toward the paper clip. Moving from the physical world to the trading world, we can substitute the prices over our window of observation for the units of weight along the ruler. Using this analogy, we see that the CG of the window moves to the right when prices increase sharply. Correspondingly, the CG of the window moves to the left when prices decrease.

The idea of computing the center of gravity arose from observing how the lags of various finite impulse response (FIR) filters vary according to the relative amplitude of the filter coefficients. A simple moving average (SMA) is an FIR filter where all the filter coefficients have the same value (usually unity). As a result, the CG of the SMA is exactly in the center of the filter. A weighted moving average (WMA) is an FIR filter where the most recent price is weighted by the length of the filter, the next most recent price is weighted by the length of the filter less 1, and so on. The weighting terms are the filter coefficients. The filter coefficients of a WMA describe the outline of a triangle. It is well known that the CG of a triangle is located at one-third the length of the base of the triangle. In other words, the CG of the WMA has shifted to the right relative to the CG of an SMA of equal length, resulting in less lag. In all FIR filters, the sum of the product of the coefficients and prices must be divided by the sum of the coefficients so that the scale of the original prices is retained.

The most general FIR filter is the Ehlers Filter,[1] which can be written as

$$\text{Ehlers Filter} = \frac{\sum\limits_{i=0}^{N} c_i * \text{Price}_i}{\sum\limits_{i=0}^{N} c_i} \tag{5.1}$$

The coefficients of the Ehlers Filter can be almost any measure of variability. I have looked at momentum, signal-to-noise ratio, volatility, and even Stochastics and Relative Strength Index (RSI) values as filter coefficients. One of the most adaptive sets of coefficients arose from video edge detection filters, and was the sum of the square of the differences between each price and each previous price. In any event, the result of using different filter coefficients is to make the filter adaptive by moving the CG of the coefficients.

While I was debugging the code of an adaptive FIR filter, I noticed that the CG itself moved in exact opposition to the price swings. The CG moves to the right when prices go up and to the left when prices go down. Measured as the distance from the most recent price, the CG decreased when prices rose and increased when they fell. All I had to do was to invert the sign of the CG to get a smoothed oscillator that was in phase with the price swings and had essentially zero lag.

The CG is computed in much the same way as we computed the Ehlers Filter. The position of the balance point is the summation of the product of position within the observation window times the price at that position divided by the summation of prices across the window. The mathematical expression for this calculation is

$$CG = \frac{\sum\limits_{i=0}^{N} (x_i + 1) * \text{Price}_i}{\sum\limits_{i=0}^{N} \text{Price}_i} \tag{5.2}$$

In this expression I added 1 to the position count because the count started with the most recent price at zero, and multiplying the most recent price by the position count would remove it from the computation. The

```
Inputs:         Price((H+L)/2),
                Length(10);

Vars:           count(0),
                Num(0),
                Denom(0),
                CG(0);

Num = 0;
Denom = 0;
For count = 0 to Length - 1 begin
        Num = Num + (1 + count)*(Price[count]);
        Denom = Denom + (Price[count]);
End;
If Denom <> 0 then CG = -Num/Denom + (Length + 1) / 2;

Plot1(CG, "CG");
Plot2(CG[1], "CG1");
```

FIGURE 5.1   EasyLanguage Code to Compute the CG Oscillator

EasyLanguage code to compute the CG Oscillator is given in Figure 5.1 and the eSignal Formula Script (EFS) code is given in Figure 5.2.

In EasyLanguage, the notation Price[N] means the price *N* bars ago. Thus Price[0] is the price for the current bar. Counting for the location is backward from the current bar. In the code the summation is accomplished by recursion, where the count is varied from the current bar to the length of the observation window. The numerator is the sum of the product of the bar position and the price, and the denominator is the sum of the prices. Then the CG is just the negative ratio of the numerator to the denominator. A zero counter value for CG is established by adding half the length of the observation window plus 1. Since the CG is smoothed, an effective crossover signal is produced simply by delaying the CG by one bar.

An example of the CG Oscillator is shown in Figure 5.3. In this case, I selected the length to be an eight-bar observation window. It is clear that every major price turning point is identified with zero lag by the CG Oscillator and the crossovers formed by its trigger. Since the CG Oscillator is filtered and smoothed, whipsaws of the crossovers are minimized. The relative amplitudes of the cyclic swings are retained. The resemblance of the CG Oscillator to the Cyber Cycle Indicator of Chapter 4 is striking. I will compare all the oscillator type indicators in a later chapter.

```
/*****************************************************
Title:      CG Oscillator
Coded By:   Chris D. Kryza (Divergence Software, Inc.)
Email:   c.kryza@gte.net
Incept:  06/27/2003
Version: 1.0.0



==========================================================
Fix History:

06/27/2003 -   Initial Release
1.0.0


==========================================================
*****************************************************/


//External Variables
var nPrice              = 0;
var nCG                 = 0;

var aPriceArray         = new Array();
var aCGArray            = new Array();


//== PreMain function required by eSignal to set_
    things up
function preMain() {
var x;

  setPriceStudy(false);
  setStudyTitle("CG Osc");
  setCursorLabelName("CG", 0);
  setCursorLabelName("Trig", 1);
  setDefaultBarFgColor( Color.blue, 0 );
  setDefaultBarFgColor( Color.red,  1 );

      //initialize arrays
  for (x=0; x<70; x++) {
      aPriceArray[x]    = 0.0;
      aCGArray[x]       = 0.0;
```

FIGURE 5.2 EFS Code to Compute the CG Oscillator

```
    }

}

//== Main processing function
function main( OscLength ) {
var x;
var nNum;
var nDenom;
var nValue1;


        //initialize parameters if necessary
        if ( OscLength == null ) {
              OscLength = 10;
        }

        // study is initializing
    if (getBarState() == BARSTATE_ALLBARS) {
      return null;
    }

        //on each new bar, save array values
        if ( getBarState() == BARSTATE_NEWBAR ) {
              aPriceArray.pop();
              aPriceArray.unshift( 0 );

              aCGArray.pop();
              aCGArray.unshift( 0 );

        }

        nPrice = ( high()+low() ) / 2;
        aPriceArray[0] = nPrice;

        nNum    = 0;
        nDenom = 0;


        for ( x=0; x<OscLength; x++ ){
              nNum += ( 1.0 + x ) * ( aPriceArray[x] );
```
                                                        (continued)

FIGURE 5.2   *(Continued)*

```
            nDenom += ( aPriceArray[x] );
    }

    if ( nDenom != 0 ) nCG = -nNum/nDenom
        + ( OscLength+1 )/2;
    aCGArray[0] = nCG;


    //return the calculated values
    if ( !isNaN( aCGArray[0] ) ) {
            return new Array( aCGArray[0],_
                aCGArray[1] );
    }


}
```

FIGURE 5.2 *(Continued)*

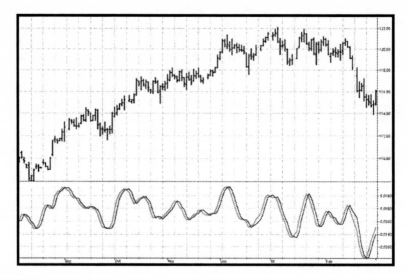

FIGURE 5.3 The CG Oscillator Accurately Identifies Each Price Turning Point

The appearance of the CG Oscillator varies with the selection of the observation window length. Ideally, the selected length should be half the dominant cycle length because half the dominant cycle fully captures the entire cyclic move in one direction. If the length is too long, the CG Oscillator is desensitized. For example, if the window length is one full dominant cycle, half the data pulls the CG to the right and the other half of the data pulls the CG to the left. As a result, the CG stays in the middle of the window and no motion of the CG Oscillator is observed. On the other hand, if the window length is too short, you are missing the benefits of smoothing. As a result of this case, the CG Oscillator contains higher-frequency components and is a little too nervous for profitable trading.

KEY POINTS TO REMEMBER

- The CG in an FIR filter is the position of the average price within the filter window length.
- The CG moves toward the most recent bar (decreases) when prices rise and moves away from the most recent bar (increases) when prices fall. Thus the CG moves exactly opposite to the price direction.
- The CG Oscillator has essentially zero lag.
- The CG Oscillator retains the relative cycle amplitude, similar to the Cyber Cycle Indicator.

CHAPTER 6

Relative Vigor Index

"Get to the back of the boat," said Tom sternly.

This chapter describing the Relative Vigor Index (RVI) uses concepts dating back over three decades and also uses modern filter and digital signal processing theory to realize those concepts as a practical and useful indicator. The RVI merges the old concepts with the new technologies. The basic idea of the RVI is that prices tend to close higher than they open in up markets and tend to close lower than they open in down markets. The vigor of the move is thus established by where the prices reside at the end of the day. To normalize the index to the daily trading range, the change in price is divided by the maximum range of prices for the day. Thus, the basic equation for the RVI is

$$RVI = \frac{Close - Open}{High - Low} \tag{6.1}$$

In 1972, Jim Waters and Larry Williams published a description of their A/D Oscillator.[1] In this case, A/D means accumulation/distribution rather than the usual advance/decline. Waters and Williams defined Buying Power (BP) and Selling Power (SP) as

$$BP = High - Open$$
$$SP = Close - Low$$

where the prices were the open, high, low, and closing prices for the day. The two values, BP and SP, show the additional buying strength relative to the open and the selling strength relative to the close to obtain an implied measure of the day's trading. Waters and Williams combined the measurement as the Daily Raw Figure (DRF). DRF is calculated as

$$DRF = \frac{BP + SP}{2 * (High - Low)} \tag{6.2}$$

The maximum value of 1 is reached when a market opens trading at the low and closes at the high. Conversely, the minimum value of 0 is reached when the market opens trading at the high and closes at the low. The day-to-day evaluation causes the DRF to vary radically and requires smoothing to make it usable.

We can expand the equation for the DRF as

$$DRF = \frac{1}{2}\left(\frac{High - Open + Close - Low}{High - Low}\right)$$

$$= \frac{1}{2}\left(\frac{High - Low + Close - Open}{High - Low}\right)$$

$$= \frac{1}{2}\left(1 + \frac{Close - Open}{High - Low}\right) \tag{6.3}$$

Clearly, the equation for the DRF is identical with the daily RVI expression except for the additive and multiplicative constants. It seems there are no new ideas in technical analysis. However, smoothing must be done to make the indicator practical. This is where modern filter theory contributes to the successful implementation of the RVI. I use the four-bar symmetrical finite impulse response (FIR) filter (described in Equation 4.1 and Figure 4.1) to independently smooth the numerator and the denominator.

The RVI is an oscillator, and we are therefore only concerned with the cycle modes of the market in its use. The sharpest rate of change for a cycle is at its midpoint. Therefore, in the ascending part of the cycle we would expect the difference between the close and open to be at a maximum. This is like a derivative in calculus, where the derivative of a sinewave produces a negative cosine wave. The derivative is therefore a waveform that leads the original sinewave by a quarter cycle. Also, from calculus, integration of a sinewave over a half-cycle period results in another sinewave delayed by a quarter cycle. Summing over a half cycle is basically the same as mathematically integrating, with the result that the waveshape of the sum is delayed by a quarter wavelength relative to the input. The net result of taking the differences and summing produces an oscillator output in phase with the cyclic component of the price. It is also possible to generate a leading function if the summation window is less than a half wavelength of the Dominant Cycle. If a cycle measurement is not available, you can sum the RVI components over a fixed default period. A nominal value of 8 is suggested because this is approximately half the period of most cycles of interest.

Calculating the RVI is straightforward. The numerator, consisting of Close – Open, is filtered in the four-bar symmetrical FIR filter before the terms are summed. The denominator, consisting of High – Low, is independently filtered in the four-bar symmetrical FIR filter before it is summed. The numerator and denominator are summed individually and the RVI is then computed as the ratio of the numerator to the denominator. Since the numerator and denominator are lagged the same amount due to filtering, the lag is removed by taking their ratio.

The rules for the use of the RVI are flexible. Just remember that it is an oscillator that is basically in phase with the cyclic component of the market prices. I prefer crossing line indicators because they are unambiguous in their signals. A simple Trigger line is just the RVI delayed by one bar.

The RVI oscillator is shown in Figure 6.1. The responsiveness and clarity of the signals are self-explanatory. The EasyLanguage code to compute the RVI is shown in Figure 6.2, and its eSignal Formula Script (EFS) code is shown in Figure 6.3.

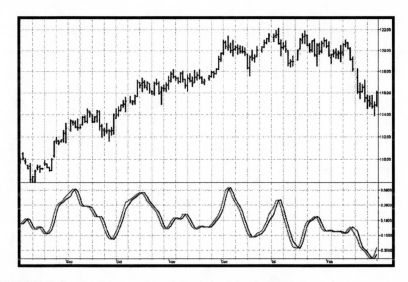

FIGURE 6.1 The RVI Gives Crisp Indications of the Cyclic Turning Point

```
Inputs:     Length(10);

Vars:       Num(0),
            Denom(0),
            count(0),
            RVI(0),
            Trigger(0);

Value1 = ((Close - Open) + 2*(Close[1]
    - Open[1]) + 2*(Close[2] - Open[2])
    + (Close[3] - Open[3]))/6;
Value2 = ((High - Low) + 2*(High[1]
    - Low[1]) + 2*(High[2] - Low[2])
    + (High[3] - Low[3]))/6;
Num = 0;
Denom = 0;
For count = 0 to Length -1 begin
            Num = Num + Value1[count];
            Denom = Denom + Value2[count];
End;
If Denom <> 0 then RVI = Num / Denom;
Trigger = RVI[1];

Plot1(RVI, "RVI");
Plot2(Trigger, "Trigger");
```

FIGURE 6.2   EasyLanguage Code to Compute the RVI

```
/*********************************************************
Title:      RVI
Coded By:   Chris D. Kryza (Divergence Software, Inc.)
Email:      c.kryza@gte.net
Incept:     06/19/2003
Version:    1.0.0


=========================================================
```

FIGURE 6.3   EFS Code to Compute the RVI

```
Fix History:

06/19/2003 -    Initial Release
1.0.0

=======================================================
*******************************************************/


//External Variables
var aRVIArray              = new Array();
var aValue1Array           = new Array();
var aValue2Array           = new Array();

//== PreMain function required by eSignal to set_
   things up
function preMain() {
var x;

    setPriceStudy(false);
    setStudyTitle("RVI");
    setCursorLabelName("RVI", 0);
    setCursorLabelName("Trig", 1);
    setDefaultBarFgColor( Color.blue, 0 );
    setDefaultBarFgColor( Color.red,  1 );
    addBand( 0, PS_SOLID, Color.black, 1, -55 );

        //initialize arrays
    for (x=0; x<70; x++) {
        aRVIArray[x]        = 0.0;
        aValue1Array[x]     = 0.0;
        aValue2Array[x]     = 0.0;
        aValue3Array[x]     = 0.0;
    }

}

//== Main processing function
function main( OscLength ) {
var x;
var nNum;
var nDenom;
                                          (continued)
```

FIGURE 6.3   *(Continued)*

```
    //initialize parameters if necessary
    if ( OscLength == null ) {
        OscLength = 8;
    }

    // study is initializing
if (getBarState() == BARSTATE_ALLBARS) {
  return null;
}

    //on each new bar, save array values
    if ( getBarState() == BARSTATE_NEWBAR ) {

        aRVIArray.pop();
        aRVIArray.unshift( 0 );

        aValue1Array.pop();
        aValue1Array.unshift( 0 );

        aValue2Array.pop();
        aValue2Array.unshift( 0 );


    }

    aValue1Array[0] = ( ( close()-open() )
        + 2*( close(-1)-open(-1) )
        + 2*( close(-2)-open(-2) )
        + ( close(-3)-open(-3) ) ) / 6;
    aValue2Array[0] = ( ( high()-low() )
        + 2*( high(-1)-low(-1) )
        + 2*( high(-2)-low(-2) )
        + ( high(-3)-low(-3) ) ) / 6;


    nNum   = 0;
    nDenom = 0;


    for ( x=0; x<OscLength; x++ ){
        nNum += aValue1Array[x];
        nDenom += aValue2Array[x];
```

FIGURE 6.3   *(Continued)*

```
        }

        if ( nDenom != 0 ) aRVIArray[0] = nNum/nDenom;


        //return the calculated values
        {
                return new Array( aRVIArray[0],_
                    aRVIArray[1] );
        }


}
```

FIGURE 6.3   *(Continued)*

KEY POINTS TO REMEMBER

- The RVI concept is that prices close higher than they open in up markets and close lower than they open in down markets.
- The RVI is a normalized oscillator, where the movement is normalized to the trading range of each bar.
- Lag-canceling four-bar symmetrical FIR filters are used to produce a readable indicator.

CHAPTER 7

Oscillator
Comparison

"Let's play musical chairs," said Tom deceitfully.

I n the previous three chapters I have described three different oscillators using three different principles. There is probably no need for
more than one oscillator in your technical trading arsenal if it is a good
one. It is my experience that a number of traders suffer from the "paralysis
of analysis." Rather than searching for the ideal combination of tools—or
worse, changing the mix of tools for every situation—it is better to settle
on the few tools that work the best for you on average. The three oscillators are for your consideration. The only way to know which of the three is
best is to do a comparison on the same chart using the same data for each.
This comparison is shown in Figure 7.1.

Frankly, I don't see a nickel's worth of difference between the three
oscillators in this particular example. All three indicate the relative cycle
amplitude and correctly identify each major turning point as it occurs. If
anything, the Relative Vigor Index (RVI) is slightly less susceptible to whipsaw indications. Nonetheless, I am partial to the Cyber Cycle because I
know it contains only the theoretical cycle components that comprise an
oscillator. I have seen greater differences between the oscillators in other
data samples.

The differences will become more apparent when you insert these
oscillators as part of an automatic trading strategy. In these applications
one oscillator may give a signal one bar earlier than the others at critical
times for the strategy. It's also true that one oscillator may have fewer
short-term crossovers that lead to whipsaw trades. In any event, you now
have three excellent tools for your own technical analysis. It may be that
one of the oscillators will outperform the others in your application.

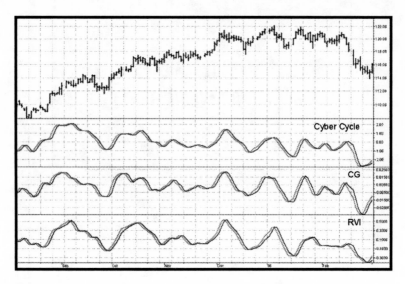

FIGURE 7.1   Comparison of the Cyber Cycle, CG, and RVI Oscillators

It may be constructive to compare just one of the oscillators I have developed to several other oscillators that are in common use on a chart using the same data as before. This standardized comparison is useful to assess the relative lag of the trading signals and the degree to which whip-saw signals are produced. Two of the more popular oscillators are the Relative Strength Index (RSI) and the Stochastic. These are compared to the Cyber Cycle in Figure 7.2, where eight-bar periods are used for comparable scaling. *Whoa!* Clearly, the RSI and Stochastic are more erratic than the Cyber Cycle. Waiting for confirmation for the indicators to cross the signal lines is the conventional way of minimizing the erratic behavior of the indicators. Waiting for confirmation means that the RSI and Stochastic trading signals are invariably late or that the signal is missed altogether. I could cite many more examples and many more comparison indicators, but the purpose of this book is to generate tools you can use in your own work. Since you have the code, you can test your own examples. You can also compare these new tools to your other favorite indicators.

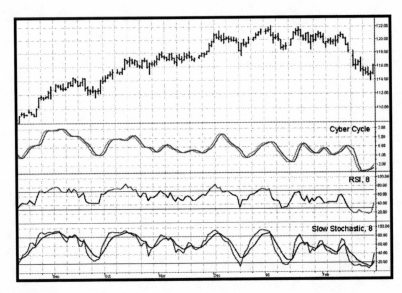

FIGURE 7.2   Cyber Cycle is Smoother and Signals are More Timely than Those of an RSI or Stochastic

KEY POINTS TO REMEMBER

- The Cyber Cycle, CG, and RVI oscillators all carry relative cycle amplitude information.
- The Cyber Cycle, CG, and RVI all indicate major turning points with minimum lag.
- The Cyber Cycle, CG, and RVI are vastly superior to standard indicators.

CHAPTER 8

Stochasticization and Fisherization of Indicators

"I'm of greater value to you every day," said Tom appreciatively.

There is an indicator I wish I had invented because it works pretty well. This indicator is called the Stochastic RSI. Since I didn't invent it, the best I can do is to describe it and then proceed to shamelessly adapt some of its principles to create even better indicators. All of these indicators will be described and compared in this chapter.

The name of the Stochastic RSI is descriptive of how it is calculated. First an RSI Indicator is computed from recent prices; then a Stochastic Indicator is computed using the RSI as the input variable. Finally, a weighted moving average of the Stochastic is taken to smooth it so that a workable output can be viewed.

An RSI averages the difference in ascending closing prices over a selected period separately from averaging the difference in descending closing prices. For a shorthand notation, I will call these Closes Up (CU) and Closes Down (CD). The RSI is the ratio of CU to the sum of CU and CD. If there are no CD in the selected period, the ratio is unity (1). If there are no CU in the selected period, the ratio is 0. So, if the length exactly coincides with half the period of a perfect cycle, the RSI will swing between 0 and 1. It is common to multiply the ratio by 100 to display the RSI as a percentage.

A Stochastic Indicator[1] (definitely not a stochastic random variable) is computed by finding the highest value and the lowest value over a selected period. The Stochastic Indicator is the ratio of the difference between the current and lowest values and the difference between the highest and lowest values. It is also common to multiply this ratio by 100 to display the Stochastic Indicator as a percentage.

The EasyLanguage and EFS codes to derive the Stochastic RSI from RSI and Stochastics are given in Figures 8.1 and 8.2, respectively. Before the Stochastic RSI is plotted, it is smoothed by a weighted moving average to provide a pleasing display with minimal lag. The Trigger line displayed is the Signal line delayed by one bar. The crossing of the Stochastic RSI Signal and a Trigger line constitutes buy and sell signals of the indicator. I have taken the liberty of scaling the Stochastic RSI to swing between –1 and +1. My scaling is selected so that I can directly apply the Fisher transform to it to generate razor-sharp entry and exit signals.

The amazing thing about the Stochastic RSI is that, after all the computations, the trading signals have almost no lag. The primary reason for this is that both the RSI and the Stochastic Indicators are ratios, so that lag in the numerator is canceled by lag in the denominator. The performance of the Stochastic RSI is shown in Figure 8.3. Unlike the Cyber Cycle and CG Oscillator, the Stochastic RSI tends not to retain the relative amplitudes of the cycles. This amplitude standardization can be an advantage to traders because it removes some of the interpretive aspects of the oscillators. In Figure 8.3, the Stochastic RSI clearly captures every major turning point in a timely manner.

This is the good part. If taking the Stochastic of a standard indicator produces a better indicator, it is reasonable that a superlative indicator can be created by applying the same process to an already good indicator. The EasyLanguage and EFS codes for transforming the Cyber Cycle of Figure 4.4 into a Stochastic Cyber Cycle are given in Figures 8.4 and 8.5, respectively. The EasyLanguage and eSignal Formula Script (EFS) codes for

```
Inputs:          RSILength(8),
                 StocLength(8),
                 WMALength(8);

Value1 = RSI(Close, RSILength) - Lowest(RSI(Close,
    RSILength), StocLength);
Value2 = Highest(RSI(Close, RSILength), StocLength)
    - Lowest(RSI(Close, RSILength), StocLength);
If Value2<>  0 then Value3 = Value1 / Value2;
Value4 = 2*(WAverage(Value3, WMALength) - .5);

Plot1(Value4, "StocRSI");
Plot2(Value4[1], "Trig");
```

FIGURE 8.1   EasyLanguage Code to Compute the Stochastic RSI

```
/*********************************************************
Title:        Stochastic RSI
Coded By:  Chris D. Kryza (Divergence Software, Inc.)
Email:  c.kryza@gte.net
Incept:  06/19/2003
Version:  1.0.0



===========================================================
Fix History:

06/19/2003 -   Initial Release
1.0.0


===========================================================
*********************************************************/


//External Variables
var nAvgUpClose            = 0;
var nAvgDnClose            = 0;
var ntAvgUpClose           = 0;
var ntAvgDnClose           = 0;
var nValue3                = 0;
var nValue4                = 0;
var nTrig                  = 0;
var bInitialized           = false;

var nRS                    = 0;
var nRSI                   = 0;

var aRSIArray              = new Array();
var aValue3Array           = new Array();


//== PreMain function required by eSignal to set_
    things up
function preMain() {
var x;

    setPriceStudy(false);
    setStudyTitle("StochasticRSI");
                                        (continued)
```

FIGURE 8.2 EFS Code to Compute the Stochastic RSI

```
    setCursorLabelName("StocRSI", 0);
    setCursorLabelName("Trig", 1);
    setDefaultBarFgColor( Color.blue, 0 );
    setDefaultBarFgColor( Color.red,  1 );

        //initialize arrays
    for (x=0; x<70; x++) {
        aRSIArray[x]    = 0.0;
        aValue3Array[x] = 0.0;
    }


}

//== Main processing function
function main( RSILength, StocLength, WMALength ) {
var x;
var nDiff;
var nDivBy;
var nValue1;
var nValue2;

        //initialize parameters if necessary
        if ( RSILength == null ) {
                RSILength = 8;
        }
        if ( StocLength == null ) {
                StocLength = 8;
        }
        if ( WMALength == null ) {
                WMALength = 8;
        }

        // study is initializing
    if (getBarState() == BARSTATE_ALLBARS) {
      return null;
    }

        //initialize the basic RSI calculation
        if ( bInitialized == false ) {
                nAvgUpClose = 0.0;
                nAvgDnClose = 0.0;
                for (x=0; x<RSILength; x++) {
```

FIGURE 8.2   *(Continued)*

```
                            nDiff = close( -x )
                               - close( -(x+1) );
                            if ( nDiff > 0 ) {
                                nAvgUpClose += nDiff;
                            }
                            else {
                                 nAvgDnClose
                                         += Math.abs
                                              ( nDiff );
                            }
                        }
                        nAvgUpClose /= RSILength;
                        nAvgDnClose /= RSILength;
                        nRS = nAvgUpClose / nAvgDnClose;
                        nRSI = 100.0 - ( 100.0 / ( 1.0
                             + nRS ) );

                        bInitialized = true;
                    }
                    //continue the RSI calculation on subsequent_
                        bars
                    else {
                            if ( getBarState() == BARSTATE_NEWBAR ) {
                                nAvgUpClose = ntAvgUpClose;
                                nAvgDnClose = ntAvgDnClose;
                                if ( !isNaN( nRSI ) ) {
                                        aRSIArray.pop();
                                        aRSIArray.unshift( 0 );
                                        aValue3Array.pop();
                                        aValue3Array.unshift( 0 );
                                        nTrig = nValue4;
                                }
                            }
                            nDiff = close( 0 ) - close( -1 );
                            if ( nDiff > 0 ) {
                                ntAvgUpClose = (( nAvgUpClose
                                    * (RSILength-1) ) + nDiff )
                                    / RSILength;
                                ntAvgDnClose = (( nAvgDnClose
                                    * (RSILength-1) ) + 0      )
                                    / RSILength;
                            }
                                                    (continued)
```

FIGURE 8.2   *(Continued)*

```
                else {
                    ntAvgUpClose = (( nAvgUpClose
                        * (RSILength-1) ) + 0      )
                        / RSILength;
                    ntAvgDnClose = (( nAvgDnClose
                        * (RSILength-1) )
                        + Math.abs( nDiff ) )
                        / RSILength;
                }
                nRS = ntAvgUpClose / ntAvgDnClose;
                nRSI = 100.0 - ( 100.0 / ( 1
                    + nRS ) );
                aRSIArray[0] = nRSI;
        }

        //calculate the StocRSI using the RSI Array we_
            have created.
        nValue1 = nRSI - Lowest( StocLength );
        nValue2 = Highest( StocLength )
            - Lowest( StocLength );

        nValue3 = 0;
        if ( nValue2 != 0 ) nValue3 = ( nValue1
            / nValue2 );
        aValue3Array[0] = nValue3;

        //compute weighted moving average
        nValue4 = 0;
        nDivBy = 0;
        for (x=0; x<WMALength; x++) {
                nValue4 += ( aValue3Array[x]
                    * ( WMALength-x ) );
                nDivBy += ( WMALength-x );
        }

        nValue4 = nValue4 / nDivBy;
        nValue4 = 2.0 * ( nValue4 - 0.5 );


        //return the calculated values
        if (!isNaN( nValue4 ) ) {
                return new Array( nValue4, nTrig );
```

FIGURE 8.2   *(Continued)*

```
        }

}


/*****************************************************
               SUPPORT FUNCTIONS
*****************************************************/


function Highest( nPeriod ) {
var x;
var nTmp = -999999999.0;

        for (x=0; x<nPeriod; x++) {
                nTmp = Math.max( nTmp, aRSIArray[x] );
        }

        return( nTmp );
}

function Lowest( nPeriod ) {
var x;
var nTmp = 999999999.0;

        for (x=0; x<nPeriod; x++) {
                nTmp = Math.min( nTmp, aRSIArray[x] );
        }

        return( nTmp );
}
```

FIGURE 8.2 *(Continued)*

converting the CG Indicator of Figure 5.3 into a Stochastic CG are given in Figures 8.6 and 8.7, respectively. Finally, the EasyLanguage and EFS codes to stochasticize the Relative Vigor Index (RVI) of Figure 6.1 are provided in Figures 8.8 and 8.9, respectively. In each case, I have simply added the code to take the Stochastic of the indicators and scaled the resulting indicators to range between −1 and +1. This scaling was done because the next step of

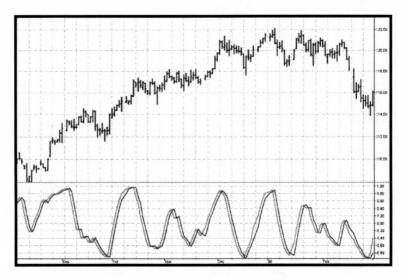

FIGURE 8.3   The Stochastic RSI Captures Turning Points in a Timely Manner

the indicator creation is to take the Fisher transform for sharper, better-defined entry and exit signals. The Trigger is just the indicator delayed by one bar and scaled to swing between –0.98 and +0.98. Shrinking the size of the Trigger gives a better-defined crossover when the indicator moves away from the extreme values.

The three stochasticized indicators are compared in Figure 8.10. They are clearly similar, although I like the Stochastic Cyber Cycle because the buy/sell indications are based purely on the cycle content of the data. On the other hand, it is clear that the Stochastic RVI is more regular with fewer whipsaws. In any event, you have all the tools to make your own selection. The input parameters for each of the indicators enable you to optimize the indicator period, if desired, when used with a specific security.

In Chapter 1, I pointed out that the probability density functions of sinewaves are not Gaussian and that creating sharp indicators from them is difficult because the indications come after the movement has already started. The Stochasticized Indicators all look somewhat like sinewaves. Therefore, we should be able to create razor-sharp trading signals by applying the Fisher transform to them. This is exactly what I have done in the indicator codes of Figures 8.11 through 8.16. I have limited the amplitude swings to absolute values of 0.99 to avoid getting huge output amplitudes from the Fisher transform. The trading signals, as before, are given by the crossing of the Signal line and the Trigger line. The Trigger line is simply the Signal line delayed by one bar.

```
{*********************************************************
                Stochastic Cyber Cycle
*******************************************************}

Inputs: Price((H+L)/2),
        alpha(.07),
        Len(8);

Vars:   Smooth(0),
        Cycle(0),
        MaxCycle(0),
        MinCycle(0);

Smooth = (Price + 2*Price[1] + 2*Price[2]
   + Price[3])/6;
Cycle = (1 - .5*alpha)*(1 - .5*alpha)*(Smooth
   - 2*Smooth[1] + Smooth[2]) + 2*(1 - alpha)*Cycle[1]
   - (1 - alpha)*(1 - alpha)*Cycle[2];
If currentbar < 7 then Cycle = (Price - 2*Price[1]
   + Price[2]) / 4;

MaxCycle = Highest(Cycle, Len);
MinCycle = Lowest(Cycle, Len);
If MaxCycle <> MinCycle then Value1 = (Cycle
   - MinCycle) / (MaxCycle - MinCycle);
Value2 = (4*Value1 + 3*Value1[1] + 2*Value1[2]
   + Value1[3]) / 10;
Value2 = 2*(Value2 - .5);

Plot1(Value2, "Cycle");
Plot2(.96*(Value2[1] + .02), "Trigger");
Plot3(0,"Ref");
```

FIGURE 8.4 EasyLanguage Code to Compute the Stochastic Cyber Cycle

```
/*********************************************************
Title:       Stochastic Cyber Cycle
Coded By:  Chris D. Kryza (Divergence Software, Inc.)
Email:   c.kryza@gte.net
Incept:   06/19/2003
                                    (continued)
```

FIGURE 8.5 EFS Code to Compute the Stochastic Cyber Cycle

```
Version:   1.0.0


=========================================================
Fix History:

06/19/2003 -    Initial Release
1.0.0


=========================================================
********************************************************/


//External Variables

var nBarCount            = 0;
var nValue2              = 0;

var aPriceArray          = new Array();
var aSmoothArray         = new Array();
var aCycleArray          = new Array();
var aValue1Array         = new Array();


//== PreMain function required by eSignal to set_
   things up
function preMain() {
var x;

  setPriceStudy(false);
  setStudyTitle("StochasticCyberCycle");
  setCursorLabelName("Cycle", 0);
  setCursorLabelName("Trig", 1);
  setDefaultBarFgColor( Color.blue, 0 );
  setDefaultBarFgColor( Color.red, 1 );
  addBand( 0, PS_SOLID, Color.black, 1, -55 );
     //initialize arrays
  for (x=0; x<70; x++) {
     aPriceArray[x]       = 0.0;
     aSmoothArray[x]      = 0.0;
     aCycleArray[x]       = 0.0;
     aValue1Array[x]      = 0.0;
```

FIGURE 8.5   *(Continued)*

```
        }

}

//== Main processing function
function main( Alpha, OscLength ) {
var x;
var nPrice;
var nMaxCycle;
var nMinCycle;

    //initialize parameters if necessary
    if ( Alpha == null ) {
            Alpha = 0.07;
    }
    if ( OscLength == null ) {
            OscLength = 8;
    }

    // study is initializing
  if (getBarState() == BARSTATE_ALLBARS) {
    return null;
  }

    //on each new bar, save array values
    if ( getBarState() == BARSTATE_NEWBAR ) {

            nBarCount++;

            aPriceArray.pop();
            aPriceArray.unshift( 0 );

            aSmoothArray.pop();
            aSmoothArray.unshift( 0 );

            aCycleArray.pop();
            aCycleArray.unshift( 0 );

            aValue1Array.pop();
            aValue1Array.unshift( 0 );
```

(continued)

FIGURE 8.5 *(Continued)*

```
                nTrig = nValue2;
     }

nPrice = ( high()+low() ) / 2;
aPriceArray[0] = nPrice;

aSmoothArray[0] = ( aPriceArray[0]
    + 2*aPriceArray[1] + 2*aPriceArray[2]
    + aPriceArray[3] ) / 6;

if ( nBarCount < 7 ) {
        aCycleArray[0] = ( aPriceArray[0]
            - 2*aPriceArray[1]
            + aPriceArray[2] ) / 4;
  }
  else {
        aCycleArray[0] = ( 1 - 0.5*Alpha ) * ( 1
        - 0.5*Alpha ) * ( aSmoothArray[0]
        - 2*aSmoothArray[1] +
        aSmoothArray[2] ) + 2*( 1-Alpha )
        * aCycleArray[1] - ( 1-Alpha )
        * ( 1- Alpha ) * aCycleArray[2];
  }

  nMaxCycle = Highest( OscLength );
  nMinCycle = Lowest( OscLength );

  if ( nMaxCycle != nMinCycle ) aValue1Array[0]
      = ( aCycleArray[0]-nMinCycle ) / ( nMaxCycle
      - nMinCycle );

  nValue2 = ( 4*aValue1Array[0]
      + 3*aValue1Array[1] + 2*aValue1Array[2]
      + aValue1Array[3] ) / 10;
  nValue2 = 2 * ( nValue2 - 0.5 );

  if (!isNaN( nValue2 ) ) {
        return new Array( nValue2,
            (0.96*(nTrig+0.02)) );
  }

}
```

FIGURE 8.5   *(Continued)*

```
/*******************************************************
                SUPPORT FUNCTIONS
*******************************************************/

function Highest( nPeriod ) {
var x;
var nTmp = -999999999.0;

        for (x=0; x<nPeriod; x++) {
                nTmp = Math.max( nTmp, aCycleArray[x] );
        }

        return( nTmp );
}

function Lowest( nPeriod ) {
var x;
var nTmp = 999999999.0;

        for (x=0; x<nPeriod; x++) {
                nTmp = Math.min( nTmp, aCycleArray[x] );
        }

        return( nTmp );
}
```

FIGURE 8.5 *(Continued)*

```
{*******************************************************
                Stochastic CG Oscillator
*******************************************************}

Inputs:  Price((H+L)/2),
         Length(8);

Vars:    count(0),
         Num(0),
         Denom(0),
         CG(0),
                                          (continued)
```

FIGURE 8.6 EasyLanguage Code to Compute the Stochastic CG

```
        MaxCG(0),
        MinCG(0);

Num = 0;
Denom = 0;
For count = 0 to Length - 1 begin
        Num = Num + (1 + count)*(Price[count]);
        Denom = Denom + (Price[count]);
End;
If Denom <> 0 then CG = -Num/Denom + (Length + 1) / 2;

MaxCG = Highest(CG, Length);
MinCG = Lowest(CG, Length);
If MaxCG <> MinCG then Value1 = (CG - MinCG) / (MaxCG
    - MinCG);
Value2 = (4*Value1 + 3*Value1[1] + 2*Value1[2]
    + Value1[3]) / 10;
Value2 = 2*(Value2 - .5);

Plot1(Value2, "CG");
Plot2(.96*(Value2[1] + .02), "Trigger");
Plot3(0,"Ref");
```

FIGURE 8.6   *(Continued)*

```
/**********************************************************
Title:          Stochastic CG Oscillator
Coded By:  Chris D. Kryza (Divergence Software, Inc.)
Email:  c.kryza@gte.net
Incept:  06/19/2003
Version:  1.0.0


==========================================================
Fix History:

06/19/2003 -    Initial Release
1.0.0
```

FIGURE 8.7   EFS Code to Compute the Stochastic CG

```
=============================================================
************************************************************/


//External Variables
var nPrice              = 0;
var nCG                 = 0;
var nValue2             = 0;
var nTrig               = 0;

var aPriceArray         = new Array();
var aCGArray            = new Array();
var aValue1Array        = new Array();


//== PreMain function required by eSignal to set_
    things up
function preMain() {
var x;

  setPriceStudy(false);
  setStudyTitle("StochasticCGOsc");
  setCursorLabelName("CG", 0);
  setCursorLabelName("Trig", 1);
  setDefaultBarFgColor( Color.blue, 0 );
  setDefaultBarFgColor( Color.red,  1 );
  addBand( 0, PS_SOLID, Color.black, 1, -55 );

          //initialize arrays
  for (x=0; x<70; x++) {
        aPriceArray[x]    = 0.0;
        aCGArray[x]       = 0.0;
        aValue1Array[x]   = 0.0;
  }


}

//== Main processing function
function main( OscLength ) {
var x;
var nNum;
var nDenom;
                                        (continued)
```

FIGURE 8.7   *(Continued)*

```
var nMaxCG;
var nMinCG;
var nValue1;


        //initialize parameters if necessary
        if ( OscLength == null ) {
             OscLength = 8;
        }

        // study is initializing
   if (getBarState() == BARSTATE_ALLBARS) {
     return null;
     }

        //on each new bar, save array values
        if ( getBarState() == BARSTATE_NEWBAR ) {
             aPriceArray.pop();
             aPriceArray.unshift( 0 );

             aCGArray.pop();
             aCGArray.unshift( 0 );

             aValue1Array.pop();
             aValue1Array.unshift( 0 );

             nTrig = nValue2;
        }

        nPrice = ( high()+low() ) / 2;
        aPriceArray[0] = nPrice;

        nNum         = 0;
        nDenom       = 0;


        for ( x=0; x<OscLength; x++ ){
             nNum += ( 1.0 + x )
                 * ( aPriceArray[x]  );
             nDenom += ( aPriceArray[x] );
        }
```

FIGURE 8.7   *(Continued)*

```
            if ( nDenom != 0 ) nCG = -nNum/nDenom
               + ( OscLength+1 )/2;
            aCGArray[0] = nCG;


            nMaxCG = Highest( OscLength);
            nMinCG = Lowest( OscLength );

            nValue1 = 0;
            if ( nMaxCG != nMinCG ) nValue1 = (nCG
               - nMinCG) / (nMaxCG - nMinCG);
            aValue1Array[0] = nValue1;

            nValue2 = ( 4*aValue1Array[0]
               + 3*aValue1Array[1] + 2*aValue1Array[2]
               + aValue1Array[3] ) / 10;
            nValue2 = 2.0 * ( nValue2 - 0.5 );

            //return the calculated values
            if ( !isNaN( nValue2 ) ) {
                return new Array( nValue2,
                    (0.96*(nTrig+0.02)) );
            }


    }



    /*********************************************************
                SUPPORT FUNCTIONS
    *********************************************************/


    function Highest( nPeriod ) {
    var x;
    var nTmp = -999999999.0;

            for (x=0; x<nPeriod; x++) {
                nTmp = Math.max( nTmp, aCGArray[x] );
            }

            return( nTmp );
```
(continued)

FIGURE 8.7   *(Continued)*

```
}

function Lowest( nPeriod ) {
var x;
var nTmp = 999999999.0;

        for (x=0; x<nPeriod; x++) {
            nTmp = Math.min( nTmp, aCGArray[x] );
        }

        return( nTmp );
}
```

FIGURE 8.7   *(Continued)*

```
{*****************************************************
            Stochastic Relative Vigor Index (RVI)
*****************************************************}
Inputs: Length(8);

Vars:   Num(0),
        Denom(0),
        count(0),
        RVI(0),
        MaxRVI(0),
        MinRVI(0);

Value1 = ((Close - Open) + 2*(Close[1] - Open[1])
    + 2*(Close[2] - Open[2]) + (Close[3] - Open[3]))/6;
Value2 = ((High - Low) + 2*(High[1] - Low[1])
    + 2*(High[2] - Low[2]) + (High[3] - Low[3]))/6;
Num = 0;
Denom = 0;
For count = 0 to Length - 1 begin
        Num = Num + Value1[count];
        Denom = Denom + Value2[count];
End;
```

FIGURE 8.8   EasyLanguage Code to Compute the Stochastic RVI

```
If Denom <> 0 then RVI = Num / Denom;

MaxRVI = Highest(RVI, Length);
MinRVI = Lowest(RVI, Length);
If MaxRVI <> MinRVI then Value3 = (RVI - MinRVI)
    / (MaxRVI - MinRVI);
Value4 = (4*Value3 + 3*Value3[1] + 2*Value3[2]
    + Value3[3]) / 10;
Value4 = 2*(Value4 - .5);

Plot1(Value4, "RVI");
Plot2(.96*(Value4[1] + .02), "Trigger");
Plot3(0,"Ref");
```

FIGURE 8.8   *(Continued)*

```
/**********************************************************
Title:        Stochastic RVI
Coded By:  Chris D. Kryza (Divergence Software, Inc.)
Email:  c.kryza@gte.net
Incept:  06/19/2003
Version:  1.0.0



==========================================================
Fix History:

06/19/2003 -    Initial Release
1.0.0


==========================================================
**********************************************************/


//External Variables
var nValue4                        = 0;
var nTrig                          = 0;
```

(continued)

FIGURE 8.9   EFS Code to Compute the Stochastic RVI

```
var aRVIArray                 = new Array();
var aValue1Array              = new Array();
var aValue2Array              = new Array();
var aValue3Array              = new Array();

//== PreMain function required by eSignal to set_
    things up
function preMain() {
var x;

  setPriceStudy(false);
  setStudyTitle("StochasticRVI");
  setCursorLabelName("RVI", 0);
  setCursorLabelName("Trig", 1);
  setDefaultBarFgColor( Color.blue, 0 );
  setDefaultBarFgColor( Color.red,  1 );
  addBand( 0, PS_SOLID, Color.black, 1, -55 );

        //initialize arrays
  for (x=0; x<70; x++) {
        aRVIArray[x]              = 0.0;
        aValue1Array[x]           = 0.0;
        aValue2Array[x]           = 0.0;
        aValue3Array[x]           = 0.0;
  }

}

//== Main processing function
function main( OscLength ) {
var x;
var nNum;
var nDenom;
var nMaxRVI;
var nMinRVI;

        //initialize parameters if necessary
        if ( OscLength == null ) {
            OscLength = 8;
        }
```

FIGURE 8.9 *(Continued)*

```
        // study is initializing
if (getBarState() == BARSTATE_ALLBARS) {
    return null;
}

        //on each new bar, save array values
        if ( getBarState() == BARSTATE_NEWBAR ) {

            aRVIArray.pop();
            aRVIArray.unshift( 0 );

            aValue1Array.pop();
            aValue1Array.unshift( 0 );

            aValue2Array.pop();
            aValue2Array.unshift( 0 );

            aValue3Array.pop();
            aValue3Array.unshift( 0 );

            nTrig = nValue4;
        }

        aValue1Array[0] = ( ( close()-open() )
            + 2*( close(-1)-open(-1) ) + 2*( close(-2)
            - open(-2) ) + ( close(-3)-open(-3) ) )
            / 6;
        aValue2Array[0] = ( ( high()-low() )
            + 2*( high(-1)-low(-1) ) + 2*( high(-2)
            - low(-2) ) + ( high(-3)-low(-3) ) ) / 6;


        nNum        = 0;
        nDenom      = 0;


        for ( x=0; x<OscLength; x++ ){
            nNum += aValue1Array[x];
            nDenom += aValue2Array[x];
        }

        if ( nDenom != 0 ) aRVIArray[0] = nNum/nDenom;
                                        (continued)
```

FIGURE 8.9   *(Continued)*

```
            nMaxRVI = Highest( OscLength);
            nMinRVI = Lowest( OscLength );

            if ( nMaxRVI != nMinRVI ) aValue3Array[0]
                = ( aRVIArray[0]-nMinRVI )
                / ( nMaxRVI-nMinRVI );

            nValue4 = ( 4*aValue3Array[0]
                + 3*aValue3Array[1] + 2*aValue3Array[2]
                + aValue3Array[3] ) / 10;
            nValue4 = 2.0 * ( nValue4 - 0.5 );

            //return the calculated values
            if ( !isNaN( nValue4 ) ) {
                return new Array( nValue4,
                    (0.96*(nTrig+0.02)) );
            }


}
/*********************************************************
            SUPPORT FUNCTIONS
*********************************************************/


function Highest( nPeriod ) {
var x;
var nTmp = -999999999.0;

        for (x=0; x<nPeriod; x++) {
            nTmp = Math.max( nTmp, aRVIArray[x] );
        }

        return( nTmp );
}

function Lowest( nPeriod ) {
var x;
var nTmp = 999999999.0;

        for (x=0; x<nPeriod; x++) {
```

FIGURE 8.9   *(Continued)*

```
             nTmp = Math.min( nTmp, aRVIArray[x] );
      }

      return( nTmp );
}
```

FIGURE 8.9 *(Continued)*

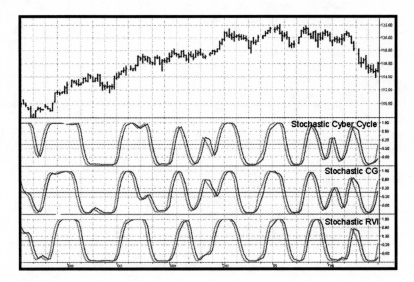

FIGURE 8.10 Comparison of the Stochasticized Indicators

```
{*****************************************************
                 Fisher Cyber Cycle
*****************************************************}
Inputs: Price((H+L)/2),
        alpha(.07),
        Len(8);

Vars:   Smooth(0),
                                          (continued)
```

FIGURE 8.11 EasyLanguage Code to Compute the Fisher Stochastic Cyber Cycle

```
        Cycle(0),
        MaxCycle(0),
        MinCycle(0),
        Lead(0);

Smooth = (Price + 2*Price[1] + 2*Price[2]
   + Price[3])/6;
Cycle = (1 - .5*alpha)*(1 - .5*alpha)*(Smooth
   - 2*Smooth[1] + Smooth[2]) + 2*(1 - alpha)*Cycle[1]
   - (1 - alpha)*(1 - alpha)*Cycle[2];
If currentbar < 7 then Cycle = (Price - 2*Price[1]
   + Price[2]) / 4;

MaxCycle = Highest(Cycle, Len);
MinCycle = Lowest(Cycle, Len);
If MaxCycle <> MinCycle then Value1 = (Cycle
   - MinCycle) / (MaxCycle - MinCycle);
Value2 = (4*Value1 + 3*Value1[1] + 2*Value1[2]
   + Value1[3]) / 10;

Value3 = .5*Log((1+1.98*(Value2-.5))/(1-1.98
   *(Value2-.5)));

Plot1(Value3, "Cycle");
Plot2(Value3[1], "Trigger");
Plot3(0,"Ref");
```

FIGURE 8.11   *(Continued)*

```
/**********************************************************
Title:        Fisher Cyber Cycle
Coded By:  Chris D. Kryza (Divergence Software, Inc.)
Email:  c.kryza@gte.net
Incept:  06/19/2003
Version:  1.0.0
```

FIGURE 8.12   EFS Code to Compute the Fisher Stochastic Cyber Cycle

```
============================================================
Fix History:
06/19/2003 -    Initial Release
1.0.0


============================================================
*******************************************************/


//External Variables

var nBarCount        = 0;
var nValue3          = 0;

var aPriceArray      = new Array();
var aSmoothArray     = new Array();
var aCycleArray      = new Array();
var aValue1Array     = new Array();


//== PreMain function required by eSignal to set
   things up
function preMain() {
var x;

  setPriceStudy(false);
  setStudyTitle("FisherCyberCycle");
  setCursorLabelName("Cycle", 0);
  setCursorLabelName("Trig", 1);
  setDefaultBarFgColor( Color.blue, 0 );
  setDefaultBarFgColor( Color.red,  1 );
  addBand( 0, PS_SOLID, Color.black, 1, -55 );

        //initialize arrays
  for (x=0; x<70; x++) {
        aPriceArray[x]    = 0.0;
        aSmoothArray[x]   = 0.0;
        aCycleArray[x]    = 0.0;
        aValue1Array[x]   = 0.0;
  }


}
                                        (continued)
```

FIGURE 8.12   *(Continued)*

```
//== Main processing function
function main( Alpha, OscLength ) {
var x;
var nPrice;
var nValue2;
var nMaxCycle;
var nMinCycle;


        //initialize parameters if necessary
        if ( Alpha == null ) {
            Alpha = 0.07;
        }
        if ( OscLength == null ) {
            OscLength = 8;
        }

        // study is initializing
    if (getBarState() == BARSTATE_ALLBARS) {
        return null;
    }

        //on each new bar, save array values
        if ( getBarState() == BARSTATE_NEWBAR ) {

            nBarCount++;

            aPriceArray.pop();
            aPriceArray.unshift( 0 );

            aSmoothArray.pop();
            aSmoothArray.unshift( 0 );

            aCycleArray.pop();
            aCycleArray.unshift( 0 );

            aValue1Array.pop();
            aValue1Array.unshift( 0 );

            nTrig = nValue3;
        }
```

FIGURE 8.12   *(Continued)*

```
nPrice = ( high()+low() ) / 2;
aPriceArray[0] = nPrice;

aSmoothArray[0] = ( aPriceArray[0]
    + 2*aPriceArray[1] + 2*aPriceArray[2]
    + aPriceArray[3] ) / 6;

if ( nBarCount < 7 ) {
    aCycleArray[0] = ( aPriceArray[0]
        - 2*aPriceArray[1]
        + aPriceArray[2] ) / 4;
}
else {
    aCycleArray[0] = ( 1 - 0.5*Alpha ) * ( 1
        - 0.5*Alpha ) * ( aSmoothArray[0]
        - 2*aSmoothArray[1] +
        aSmoothArray[2] ) + 2*( 1-Alpha )
        * aCycleArray[1] - ( 1-Alpha )
        * ( 1-Alpha ) * aCycleArray[2];
}

nMaxCycle = Highest( OscLength );
nMinCycle = Lowest( OscLength );

if ( nMaxCycle != nMinCycle ) aValue1Array[0]
    = ( aCycleArray[0]-nMinCycle )
    / ( nMaxCycle - nMinCycle );

nValue2 = ( 4*aValue1Array[0]
    + 3*aValue1Array[1] + 2*aValue1Array[2]
    + aValue1Array[3] ) / 10;
nValue3 = 0.5 * Math.log( ( 1 + 1.98
    * ( nValue2-0.5 ) ) / ( 1 - 1.98
    * ( nValue2-0.5 ) ) );

//return the calculated values
if (!isNaN( nValue3 ) ) {
    return new Array( nValue3, nTrig );
}


}
```

(continued)

FIGURE 8.12 *(Continued)*

```
/********************************************************
               SUPPORT FUNCTIONS
 ********************************************************/


function Highest( nPeriod ) {
var x;
var nTmp = -999999999.0;

       for (x=0; x<nPeriod; x++) {
              nTmp = Math.max( nTmp, aCycleArray[x] );
       }

        return( nTmp );
}

function Lowest( nPeriod ) {
var x;
var nTmp = 999999999.0;

       for (x=0; x<nPeriod; x++) {
              nTmp = Math.min( nTmp, aCycleArray[x] );
       }

       return( nTmp );
}
```

FIGURE 8.12   *(Continued)*

```
{*******************************************************
                      Fisher CG
********************************************************}
Inputs: Price((H+L)/2),
        Length(8);

Vars:   count(0),
        Num(0),
        Denom(0),
        CG(0),
        MaxCG(0),
        MinCG(0),
        Lead(0);

Num = 0;
Denom = 0;
For count = 0 to Length - 1 begin
        Num = Num + (1 + count)*(Price[count]);
        Denom = Denom + (Price[count]);
End;
If Denom <> 0 then CG = -Num/Denom + (Length + 1) / 2;

MaxCG = Highest(CG, Length);
MinCG = Lowest(CG, Length);
If MaxCG <> MinCG then Value1 = (CG - MinCG) /
    (MaxCG - MinCG);
Value2 = (4*Value1 + 3*Value1[1] + 2*Value1[2] +
    Value1[3]) / 10;

Value3 = .5*Log((1+1.98*(Value2-.5))/(1-1.98
    *(Value2-.5)));

Plot1(Value3, "CG");
Plot2(Value3[1], "Trigger");
Plot3(0,"Ref");
```

FIGURE 8.13   EasyLanguage Code to Compute the Fisher Stochastic CG

```
/*******************************************************
Title:         Fisher Stochastic CG Oscillator
Coded By:      Chris D. Kryza (Divergence Software, Inc.)
Email:         c.kryza@gte.net
Incept:        06/19/2003
Version:       1.0.0


=======================================================
Fix History:

06/19/2003 -   Initial Release
1.0.0

=======================================================
*******************************************************/


//External Variables
var nPrice              = 0;
var nCG                 = 0;
var nValue3             = 0;
var nTrig               = 0;

var aPriceArray              = new Array();
var aCGArray                 = new Array();
var aValue1Array             = new Array();

//== PreMain function required by eSignal to set_
   things up
function preMain() {
var x;

  setPriceStudy(false);
  setStudyTitle("FisherStochasticCGOsc");
  setCursorLabelName("CG", 0);
  setCursorLabelName("Trig", 1);
  setDefaultBarFgColor( Color.blue, 0 );
  setDefaultBarFgColor( Color.red,  1 );
  addBand( 0, PS_SOLID, Color.black, 1, -55 );
```

FIGURE 8.14   EFS Code to Compute the Fisher Stochastic CG

```
        //initialize arrays
  for (x=0; x<70; x++) {
        aPriceArray[x]     = 0.0;
        aCGArray[x]        = 0.0;
        aValue1Array[x]    = 0.0;
  }


}

//== Main processing function
function main( OscLength ) {
var x;
var nNum;
var nDenom;
var nMaxCG;
var nMinCG;
var nValue1;

        //initialize parameters if necessary
        if ( OscLength == null ) {
             OscLength = 8;
        }

        // study is initializing
  if (getBarState() == BARSTATE_ALLBARS) {
        return null;
  }

        //on each new bar, save array values
        if ( getBarState() == BARSTATE_NEWBAR ) {
             aPriceArray.pop();
             aPriceArray.unshift( 0 );

             aCGArray.pop();
             aCGArray.unshift( 0 );

             aValue1Array.pop();
             aValue1Array.unshift( 0 );

                                          (continued)
```

FIGURE 8.14 *(Continued)*

```
        nTrig = nValue3;
    }

    nPrice = ( high()+low() ) / 2;
    aPriceArray[0] = nPrice;

    nNum        = 0;
    nDenom      = 0;


    for ( x=0; x<OscLength; x++ ){
        nNum += ( 1.0 + x )
            * ( aPriceArray[x] );
        nDenom += ( aPriceArray[x] );
    }

    if ( nDenom != 0 ) nCG = -nNum/nDenom
        + ( OscLength+1 )/2;
    aCGArray[0] = nCG;

    nMaxCG = Highest( OscLength);
    nMinCG = Lowest( OscLength );

    if ( nMaxCG != nMinCG ) aValue1Array[0]
        = (nCG - nMinCG) / (nMaxCG - nMinCG);

    nValue2 = ( 4*aValue1Array[0]
        + 3*aValue1Array[1] + 2*aValue1Array[2]
        + aValue1Array[3] ) / 10;
    nValue3 = 0.5 * Math.log( ( 1 + 1.98
        * ( nValue2-0.5 ) ) / ( 1 - 1.98
        * ( nValue2-0.5 ) ) );

    //return the calculated values
    if ( !isNaN( nValue3 ) ) {
        return new Array( nValue3, nTrig );
    }


}
```

FIGURE 8.14   *(Continued)*

```
/ * * * * * * * * * * * * * * * * * * * * * * * * * * * * * * * * * * * * * * * * * * * * *
                SUPPORT FUNCTIONS
* * * * * * * * * * * * * * * * * * * * * * * * * * * * * * * * * * * * * * * * * * * * * * /


function Highest( nPeriod ) {
var x;
var nTmp = -999999999.0;

        for (x=0; x<nPeriod; x++) {
                nTmp = Math.max( nTmp, aCGArray[x] );
        }

        return( nTmp );
}

function Lowest( nPeriod ) {
var x;
var nTmp = 999999999.0;

        for (x=0; x<nPeriod; x++) {
                nTmp = Math.min( nTmp, aCGArray[x] );
        }

        return( nTmp );
}
```

FIGURE 8.14 *(Continued)*

```
{ * * * * * * * * * * * * * * * * * * * * * * * * * * * * * * * * * * * * * * * * * * * * *
                        Fisher RVI
* * * * * * * * * * * * * * * * * * * * * * * * * * * * * * * * * * * * * * * * * * * * * * }


Inputs: Length(8);

Vars:   Num(0),
        Denom(0),
        count(0),
                                                (continued)
```

FIGURE 8.15 EasyLanguage Code to Compute the Fisher Stochastic RVI

```
        RVI(0),
        Lead(0),
        MaxRVI(0),
        MinRVI(0);

Value1 = ((Close - Open) + 2*(Close[1] - Open[1])
   + 2*(Close[2] - Open[2]) + (Close[3] - Open[3]))/6;
Value2 = ((High - Low) + 2*(High[1] - Low[1])
   + 2*(High[2] - Low[2]) + (High[3] - Low[3]))/6;
Num = 0;
Denom = 0;
For count = 0 to Length - 1 begin
        Num = Num + Value1[count];
        Denom = Denom + Value2[count];
End;
If Denom <> 0 then RVI = Num / Denom;

MaxRVI = Highest(RVI, Length);
MinRVI = Lowest(RVI, Length);
If MaxRVI <> MinRVI then Value3 = (RVI - MinRVI)
   / (MaxRVI - MinRVI);
Value4 = (4*Value3 + 3*Value3[1] + 2*Value3[2]
   + Value3[3]) / 10;

Value5 = .5*Log((1+1.98*(Value4 - .5))/(1-1.98*(Value4
   - .5)));

Plot1(Value5, "RVI");
Plot2(Value5[1], "Trigger");
Plot3(0,"Ref");
```

FIGURE 8.15 *(Continued)*

```
/*********************************************************
Title:      FisherStochastic RVI
Coded By:  Chris D. Kryza (Divergence Software, Inc.)
Email:  c.kryza@gte.net
Incept:  06/19/2003
Version:  1.0.0



=======================================================
Fix History:

06/19/2003 -   Initial Release
1.0.0



=======================================================
*********************************************************/


//External Variables
var nValue5           = 0;
var nTrig             = 0;

var aRVIArray         = new Array();
var aValue1Array      = new Array();
var aValue2Array      = new Array();
var aValue3Array      = new Array();

//== PreMain function required by eSignal to set_
   things up
function preMain() {
var x;

  setPriceStudy(false);
  setStudyTitle("FisherStochasticRVI");
  setCursorLabelName("RVI", 0);
  setCursorLabelName("Trig", 1);
  setDefaultBarFgColor( Color.blue, 0 );
  setDefaultBarFgColor( Color.red, 1 );
  addBand( 0, PS_SOLID, Color.black, 1, -55 );

          //initialize arrays
  for (x=0; x<70; x++) {
```
(continued)

FIGURE 8.16 EFS Code to Compute the Fisher Stochastic RVI

```
        aRVIArray[x]            = 0.0;
        aValue1Array[x]         = 0.0;
        aValue2Array[x]         = 0.0;
        aValue3Array[x]         = 0.0;
    }

}

//== Main processing function
function main( OscLength ) {
var x;
var nNum;
var nDenom;
var nValue4;
var nMaxRVI;
var nMinRVI;


        //initialize parameters if necessary
        if ( OscLength == null ) {
            OscLength = 8;
        }

        // study is initializing
    if (getBarState() == BARSTATE_ALLBARS) {
        return null;
    }

        //on each new bar, save array values
        if ( getBarState() == BARSTATE_NEWBAR ) {

            aRVIArray.pop();
            aRVIArray.unshift( 0 );

            aValue1Array.pop();
            aValue1Array.unshift( 0 );

            aValue2Array.pop();
            aValue2Array.unshift( 0 );

            aValue3Array.pop();
            aValue3Array.unshift( 0 );
```

FIGURE 8.16   (Continued)

```
        nTrig = nValue5;
    }

    aValue1Array[0] = ( ( close()-open() )
        + 2*( close(-1)-open(-1) )
        + 2*( close(-2)-open(-2) )
        + ( close(-3)-open(-3) ) ) / 6;
    aValue2Array[0] = ( ( high()-low() )
        + 2*( high(-1)-low(-1) )
        + 2*( high(-2)-low(-2) )
        + ( high(-3)-low(-3) ) ) / 6;


    nNum        = 0;
    nDenom      = 0;


    for ( x=0; x<OscLength; x++ ){
        nNum += aValue1Array[x];
        nDenom += aValue2Array[x];
    }

    if ( nDenom != 0 ) aRVIArray[0] = nNum/nDenom;
    nMaxRVI = Highest( OscLength);
    nMinRVI = Lowest( OscLength );

    if ( nMaxRVI != nMinRVI ) aValue3Array[0]
        = ( aRVIArray[0]-nMinRVI )
        / ( nMaxRVI-nMinRVI );

    nValue4 = ( 4*aValue3Array[0]
        + 3*aValue3Array[1] + 2*aValue3Array[2]
        + aValue3Array[3] ) / 10;
    nValue5 = 0.5 * Math.log( ( 1 + 1.98
        * ( nValue4-0.5 ) ) / ( 1 - 1.98
        * ( nValue4-0.5 ) ) );

    //return the calculated values
    if ( !isNaN( nValue5 ) ) {
        return new Array( nValue5, nTrig );
    }


}
```
(continued)

FIGURE 8.16 *(Continued)*

```
/*****************************************************
            SUPPORT FUNCTIONS
*****************************************************/


function Highest( nPeriod ) {
var x;
var nTmp = -999999999.0;

        for (x=0; x<nPeriod; x++) {
             nTmp = Math.max( nTmp, aRVIArray[x] );
        }

        return( nTmp );
}

function Lowest( nPeriod ) {
var x;
var nTmp = 999999999.0;

        for (x=0; x<nPeriod; x++) {
             nTmp = Math.min( nTmp, aRVIArray[x] );
        }

        return( nTmp );
}
```

FIGURE 8.16   *(Continued)*

The three Fisherized indicators are compared in Figure 8.17. In all cases, the Fisher transform provides a means to filter the undesired whipsaw signals by ignoring line crossovers that happen at an absolute amplitude of less than 2. It appears that the Fisher RVI is the superior oscillator because, almost without exception, it provides trading signals several bars in advance of the other indicators. That makes it a *really* good indicator because the other two are not slouches in their own right. Any or all of the three can be a profound addition to your technical analysis tools.

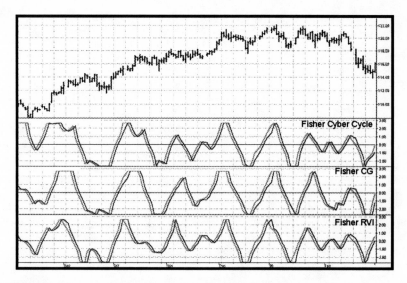

FIGURE 8.17 Fisherized Indicators Give Razor-Sharp Trading Signals

KEY POINTS TO REMEMBER

- New, easier-to-read oscillators can be created by applying the Stochastic calculation to existing indicators.
- The Stochastic RVI is an extraordinarily smooth and consistent oscillator.
- Performing a Fisher transform on amplitude-limited oscillators provides a way to eliminate whipsaw signals by ignoring crossovers that occur at amplitudes less than 2.
- The Fisher RSI provides consistently timely signals with surgical precision.

CHAPTER 9

Measuring Cycles

"Looks like rain," said Tom precipitously.

I t is obvious that cycles exist in the market. They can be found on any chart by the most casual observer. What is not so clear is how to identify those cycles in real time and how to take advantage of their existence. When Welles Wilder first introduced the Relative Strength Index (RSI), I was curious as to why he selected 14 bars as the basis of his calculations. I reasoned that if I knew the correct market conditions, then I could make indicators such as the RSI adaptive to those conditions. Cycles were the answer. I knew cycles could be measured. Once I had the cyclic measurement, a host of automatically adaptive indicators could follow.

Measurement of market cycles is not easy. The signal-to-noise ratio is often very low, making measurement difficult even using a good measurement technique. Additionally, the measurements theoretically involve simultaneously solving a triple infinity of parameter values. The parameters required for the general solutions were frequency, amplitude, and phase. Some standard engineering tools, like fast Fourier transforms (FFTs), are simply not appropriate for measuring market cycles because FFTs cannot simultaneously meet the stationarity constraints and produce results with reasonable resolution. Therefore I introduced Maximum Entropy Spectral Analysis (MESA) for the measurement of market cycles. This approach, originally developed to interpret seismographic information for oil exploration, produces high-resolution outputs with an exceptionally short amount of information. A short data length improves the probability of having nearly stationary data. Stationary data means that frequency and amplitude are constant over the length of the data. I noticed over the years that the cycles were ephemeral. Their periods would be

continuously increasing and decreasing. Their amplitudes also were changing, giving variable signal-to-noise ratio conditions. Although all this is
going on with the cyclic components, the enduring characteristic is that
generally only one tradable cycle at a time is present for the data set being
used. I prefer the term *Dominant Cycle* to denote that one component. The
assumption that there is only one cycle in the data collapses the difficulty
of the measurement process dramatically.

Assuming that only one cycle is present in the data enables the measurement to be made using a frequency discriminator. A frequency discriminator basically measures the differential phase between successive samples.
Since there are 360 degrees in each cycle, dividing 360 by the differential
phase produces the measured cycle length. For example, if the differential
phase is 20°, the resulting cycle length would be 360/20 = 18 bars. That is, an
18-bar cycle is changing phase at the rate of 20° per sample so that 360° (one
cycle) is reached after 18 samples. Pretty simple! The most significant fact is
that, in theory, the cycle measurement can be attained in just two samples.

To make the phase measurements, we need to describe the cycle in
terms of a phasor instead of the conventional waveform with which we are
familiar. The relationship between the cycle waveform and the phasor is
shown in Figure 9.1. Imagine the phasor as the arrow whose tail is pinned
at the origin and is rotating counterclockwise. A shadow cast by the arrow-
head would then trace out the sinewave cycle. That is, as the phasor
rotates, the peak amplitude is reached, followed by the zero crossing, followed by the minimum cycle amplitude, and then back to zero, and so on.
One complete rotation of the phasor describes a cycle.

The phasor can be broken into two components, called the InPhase
and Quadrature components, as shown in Figure 9.2. The phase angle for
any given sample is easily found as the arctangent of the ratio of these two
components.

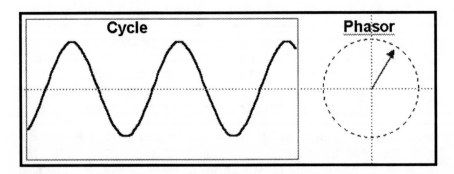

FIGURE 9.1   A Phasor Can Represent a Cycle

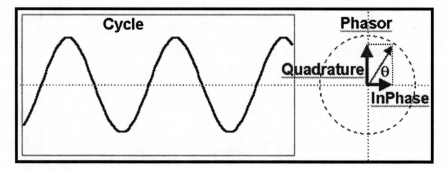

FIGURE 9.2 The Phase Angle Is the Arctangent of the Ratio of the Quadrature and InPhase Components

The trick is to break the analytic waveform (the cyclic component of prices in the form with which we are familiar) into the InPhase and Quadrature components. This is done with the Hilbert transform.[1] The Hilbert transform is theoretically an infinite series; to make it practical for traders I have truncated the series at four elements. The equation for the Quadrature component in EasyLanguage notation is

$$Q = 0.0962 * Price + 0.5769 * Price[2] - 0.5769 \\ * Price[4] - 0.0962 * Price[6]; \tag{9.1}$$

The lag of the Quadrature component is half the filter length, or three bars. Therefore the InPhase component is just the price delayed by three bars, or

$$I = Price[3]; \tag{9.2}$$

To test the speed of the cycle-measuring process, I created a single cycle of a 20-bar sinewave. I then applied the Hilbert transform, computed the phase angles, and used a discriminator to measure the cycle period. The results of this experiment are shown in Figure 9.3. These results are impressive. An accurate measurement of the cycle period is made within four samples of the beginning of the cycle. That four-sample lag is just the lag of the Hilbert transform plus one more sample because the phase difference between samples is required for the computation of the period.

Before getting too excited about these results, please recall that this is a purely monochromatic theoretical waveform having an infinite signal-to-noise ratio. Furthermore, the waveform is already detrended because the cycle swings about the zero line. In the real world we must

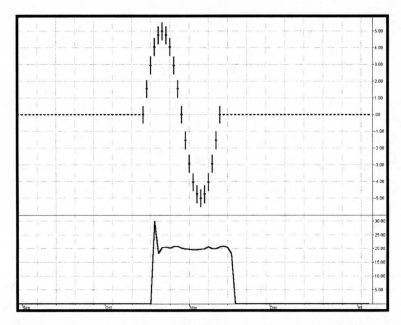

FIGURE 9.3   The Hilbert Transform Enables Rapid Measurement of the Cycle Period

detrend the signal to extract the cyclic component and then also deal with the noise that is superimposed on the signal. In other words, we need to compute the cyclic component of the market prices as we did in Figure 4.2 before we compute the cycle period.

The EasyLanguage and eSignal Formula Script (EFS) codes for computing the cycle period are shown in Figures 9.4 and 9.5, respectively. The description of the calculation is done with reference to Figure 9.4. After defining the inputs and declaring the variables, the first three lines of code recover the cyclic component, just as in Figure 4.2. The cyclic component is used to compute the Quadrature (Q1) and InPhase (I1) components of the Hilbert transform. One penalty for truncating the infinite series in computing the Quadrature component is that its amplitude is attenuated for the longer cycle periods. The last term in the computation of Q1 is a straight-line amplitude correction. Since the period is not yet known at this point in the code, and since the period is a relatively slowly varying function from sample to sample, it is satisfactory to use the period computed one bar ago in this compensation. I found this feedback compensation to be the most robust approach.

There is another amplitude compensation scheme that is possible. In the case of a pure cycle I can think of the InPhase component being Cos (θ)

```
Inputs:              Price((H+L)/2),
                     alpha(.07);

Vars:                Smooth(0),
                     Cycle(0),
                     Q1(0),
                     I1(0),
                     DeltaPhase(0),
                     MedianDelta(0),
                     DC(0),
                     InstPeriod(0),
                     Period(0),
                     I2(0),
                     Q2(0);

Smooth = (Price + 2*Price[1] + 2*Price[2]
    + Price[3])/6;
Cycle = (1 - .5*alpha)*(1 - .5*alpha)*(Smooth
    - 2*Smooth[1] + Smooth[2]) + 2*(1 - alpha)*Cycle[1]
    - (1 - alpha)*(1 - alpha)*Cycle[2];
If currentbar < 7 then Cycle = (Price - 2*Price[1]
    + Price[2]) / 4;

Q1 = (.0962*Cycle + .5769*Cycle[2] - .5769*Cycle[4]
    - .0962*Cycle[6])*(.5 + .08*InstPeriod[1]);
I1 = Cycle[3];

If Q1 <> 0 and Q1[1] <> 0 then DeltaPhase = (I1/Q1
    - I1[1]/Q1[1]) / (1 + I1*I1[1]/(Q1*Q1[1]));
If DeltaPhase < 0.1 then DeltaPhase = 0.1;
If DeltaPhase > 1.1 then DeltaPhase = 1.1;
MedianDelta = Median(DeltaPhase, 5);

If MedianDelta = 0 then DC = 15 else DC
    = 6.28318 / MedianDelta + .5;

InstPeriod = .33*DC + .67*InstPeriod[1];
Period = .15*InstPeriod + .85*Period[1];


Plot1(Period, "Period");
```

FIGURE 9.4 EasyLanguage Code to Compute the Cycle Period

```
/********************************************************
Title:        Cycle Period
Coded By:     Chris D. Kryza (Divergence Software, Inc.)
Email:        c.kryza@gte.net
Incept:       06/19/2003
Version:      1.0.0



========================================================
Fix History:

06/19/2003 -   Initial Release
1.0.0


========================================================
********************************************************/


//External Variables

var nBarCount          = 0;

var aPriceArray        = new Array();
var aSmoothArray       = new Array();
var aCycleArray        = new Array();
var aDeltaPhase        = new Array();
var aPeriod            = new Array();
var aInstPeriod        = new Array();
var aQ1                = new Array();
var aI1                = new Array();


//== PreMain function required by eSignal to set_
   things up
function preMain() {
var x;

  setPriceStudy(false);
  setStudyTitle("Cycle Period");
  setCursorLabelName("Period", 0);
  setDefaultBarFgColor( Color.blue, 0 );
```

FIGURE 9.5 EFS Code to Compute the Cycle Period

```
      //initialize arrays
   for (x=0; x<10; x++) {
       aPriceArray[x]    = 0.0;
       aSmoothArray[x]   = 0.0;
       aCycleArray[x]    = 0.0;
       aQ1[x]            = 0.0;
       aI1[x]            = 0.0;
       aDeltaPhase[x]    = 0.0;
       aPeriod[x]        = 0.0;
       aInstPeriod[x]    = 0.0;
   }


}

//== Main processing function
function main( Alpha ) {
var x;
var nDC;
var nMedianDelta;

      //initialize parameters if necessary
      if ( Alpha == null ) {
              Alpha = 0.07;
      }

      // study is initializing
    if ( getBarState() == BARSTATE_ALLBARS ) {
       return null;
    }

      //on each new bar, save array values
      if ( getBarState() == BARSTATE_NEWBAR ) {

              nBarCount++;

              aPriceArray.pop();
              aPriceArray.unshift( 0 );

              aSmoothArray.pop();
              aSmoothArray.unshift( 0 );

                                              (continued)
```

FIGURE 9.5 *(Continued)*

```
                    aCycleArray.pop();
                    aCycleArray.unshift( 0 );

                    aQ1.pop();
                    aQ1.unshift( 0 );

                    aI1.pop();
                    aI1.unshift( 0 );

                    aDeltaPhase.pop();
                    aDeltaPhase.unshift( 0 );

                    aInstPeriod.pop();
                    aInstPeriod.unshift( 0 );

                    aPeriod.pop();
                    aPeriod.unshift( 0 );


          }

          aPriceArray[0] = ( high()+low() ) / 2;

          aSmoothArray[0] = ( aPriceArray[0]
             + 2*aPriceArray[1] + 2*aPriceArray[2]
             + aPriceArray[3] ) / 6;

          if ( nBarCount < 7 ) {
                    aCycleArray[0] = ( aPriceArray[0]
                       - 2*aPriceArray[1]
                       + aPriceArray[2] ) / 4;
          }
          else {
                    aCycleArray[0] = ( 1 - 0.5*Alpha )
                       * ( 1 - 0.5*Alpha )
                       * ( aSmoothArray[0]
                       - 2*aSmoothArray[1]
                       + aSmoothArray[2] ) + 2*( 1-Alpha )
                       * aCycleArray[1] - ( 1-Alpha )
                       * ( 1-Alpha ) * aCycleArray[2];
          }
```

FIGURE 9.5   *(Continued)*

```
    aQ1[0] = ( 0.0962*aCycleArray[0]
        + 0.5769*aCycleArray[2]
        - 0.5769*aCycleArray[4]
        - 0.0962*aCycleArray[6] ) * ( 0.5 + 0.08
        * aInstPeriod[1] );
    aI1[0] = aCycleArray[3];

    if ( aQ1[0] != 0 && aQ1[1] != 0 ) {
        aDeltaPhase[0] = (aI1[0]/aQ1[0]
            - aI1[1]/aQ1[1]) / (1
            + aI1[0]*aI1[1]/(aQ1[0]*aQ1[1]));
    }
    if ( aDeltaPhase[0] < 0.1 ) aDeltaPhase[0]
        = 0.1;
    if ( aDeltaPhase[0] > 1.1 ) aDeltaPhase[0]
        = 1.1;
    //Need a 5 bar Median filter of DeltaPhase here_
        (MedianDelta)
    nMedianDelta = Median( 5, aDeltaPhase );

    if ( nMedianDelta == 0 ) {
        nDC = 15;
    }
    else {
        nDC = 6.28318 / nMedianDelta + 0.5;
    }

    aInstPeriod[0] = 0.33 * nDC + 0.67
        * aInstPeriod[1];
    aPeriod[0] = 0.15*aInstPeriod[0]
        + 0.85*aPeriod[1];

    return( aPeriod[0] );


}



function Median( nBars, aArray ) {
var aTmp = new Array();
                                            (continued)
```

FIGURE 9.5 *(Continued)*

```
var nTmp;
var result;
var x;

      //transfer elements to temp array
      x = 0;
      while( x < nBars ) {
              aTmp[x] = aArray[x++];
      }
      //sort array in asc order
      aTmp.sort( SortAsc );


      //if odd # of elements, just take middle
      if ( nBars % 2 != 0 ) {
              result = aTmp[ (nBars+1) / 2 ]
              aTmp = null;
              return( result );
      }
      //if even # elements, take average of two_
         middle elements
      else {
              nTmp = nBars/2;
              result = (aTmp[nTmp] + aTmp[nTmp+1])/2;
              aTmp = null;
              return ( result );
      }
}


function SortAsc( arg1, arg2 ) {
        if (arg1<arg2) {
           return( -1 )
        }
        else {
           return( 1 );
        }
}
```

FIGURE 9.5   *(Continued)*

and the Quadrature component being Sin (θ). Then, a compensation for amplitude error in the Quadrature component can be computed from the simple trigonometric identity

$$\mathrm{Sin}^2(\theta) = 1 - \mathrm{Cos}^2(\theta)$$

and normalizing amplitudes. While this is a great theory, and it works on theoretical waveforms, I could not obtain satisfactory compensation on real price data because of the noise present in that data. I therefore use the feedback amplitude compensation in the code.

The computation of the DeltaPhase starts with a conditional IF statement to preclude the possibility of dividing by 0. Some explanation for the rest of the line is required. The phase angle measured for the current bar is ArcTan (I1/Q1) and the phase angle for one bar ago is ArcTan (I1[1]/Q1[1]). The differential phase calculation is simplified using the trigonometric identity

$$\mathrm{ArcTan}\ (A) - \mathrm{ArcTan}(B) = \mathrm{ArcTan}\left(\frac{A-B}{1+AB}\right) \qquad (9.3)$$

A six-bar cycle is as short as we need to measure. A six-bar cycle has a phase shift of 60° per bar, or 1.047 radians per bar. Since the differential phase has a maximum of about one radian, a reasonable approximation is that the angle in radians is approximately equal to the arctangent of that angle. This is the approximation we have applied to the computation of the differential angle in the code.

After the DeltaPhase is first computed, some limits must be established. First, the DeltaPhase must always be positive because time cannot run backward. If we get a negative DeltaPhase computation, it is either due to noise or because the two absolute phase measurements have split a quadrant of the phasor. (The arctangent is positive in quadrants 1 and 3 and is negative in quadrants 2 and 4.) In the case of a negative DeltaPhase, it is satisfactory to substitute the previous calculation. Instead, if the DeltaPhase is less than 0.1 radians I limit it to 0.1 radians. This is because a DeltaPhase smaller than 0.1 radians implies the period is greater than 63 bars (2 * π/0.1). The other limit is to not compute a period of less than six bars. This is done by limiting the DeltaPhase to 1.1 radians.

The actual calculation of the cycle period is perhaps the easiest part of the code to understand. In a nutshell, the concept is to divide the DeltaPhase into 2π because 2π represents one full cycle of phases in radian measure. In practice, DeltaPhase is very noisy, varying by a large amount from bar to bar. If DeltaPhase were used directly, substantial smoothing would be required to recover a reasonable Dominant Cycle. There is a more efficient way of smoothing. The best kind of filter to use on spiky data is a median filter. Therefore I filter the DeltaPhases over five samples in a median filter to give the variable MedianDelta. MedianDelta is then divided into 2π to compute the Dominant Cycle. Measuring theoretical sinewave periods, I found there is a bias of about 0.5 in the period measurement, and therefore added a compensation term to remove that bias. The Dominant Cycle is smoothed in an exponential moving average having $\alpha = 0.33$ for a relatively rapid response for the feedback term in the computation of Q1. I call this variable the Instantaneous Period (InstPeriod). The InstPeriod is then smoothed again in an exponential moving average having $\alpha = 0.15$. This value was selected to reach the full cycle length measurement in one cycle of a 20-bar signal, starting from 0.

I have conducted a number of rigorous tests to examine the quality of the cycle measurement. First among these is to examine the start-up transient in a way similar to the single cycle measurement of Figure 9.3. The final results are shown in the bottom subgraph of Figure 9.6. In this case, I continue the 20-bar cycles after the first one. The InstPeriod comes up to a 20-bar measurement at 8 bars after initiation. This is consistent with the 1.5-bar lag of the smoothing filter plus the four-bar lag for the Hilbert

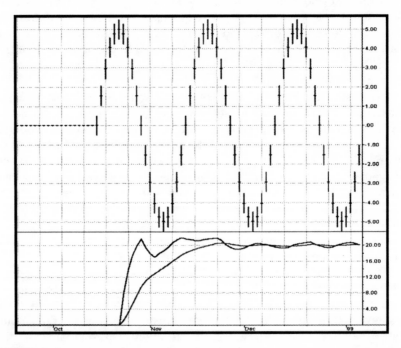

FIGURE 9.6 Measurement of a Single 20-Bar Cycle

transform plus the 2.5-bar lag of the median filter. The smoothing of the period output is due to the exponential moving average. I could have used less smoothing. However, cycle periods tend to change relatively slowly in real data, and the greater amount of smoothing is desirable when lag is of less concern. These results should be viewed in context. For example, an FFT would take about 16 cycles of data to make a measurement of comparable resolution. Yes, you read it correctly—16 full cycles of data would be required by an FFT for equivalent results. Even MESA would take a large fraction of the cycle to make the first measurement.

With any measurement algorithm, one crucial test is whether the algorithm makes a correct measurement over a wide range of input data. To this end I created a theoretical sinewave whose period gradually increased from 6 bars to 40 bars. Figure 9.7 shows this waveform and shows that the measurement of its cycle periods is very accurate.

Another transient and accuracy test is to measure how fast the measurement algorithm can follow the switch from a 30-bar cycle to a 15-bar cycle and back. In Figure 9.8, the data consists of two cycles of a 30-bar

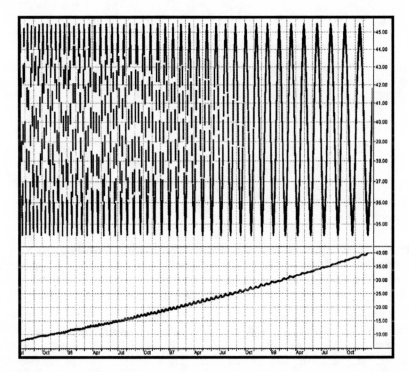

FIGURE 9.7   Measurement of a Chirped Waveform Whose Period Increases from 6 Bars to 40 Bars

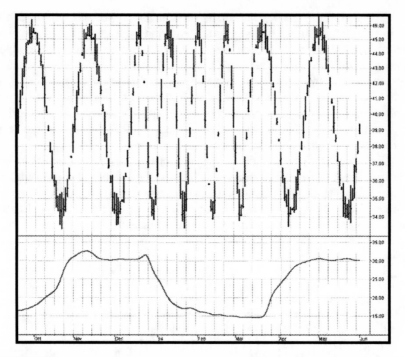

FIGURE 9.8   Measurement of Cycle Periods Varying from 30-Bar Cycles to 15-Bar Cycles and Back

cycle, four cycles of a 15-bar cycle, and two more cycles of a 30-bar cycle. This is a severe test, requiring the measurement to slew over a wide range between harmonically related cycles. This test shows that the measurement is within reasonable range of the actual period within 15 samples, switching either way.

The basic message here is that the cycle measurement has a lag of about 8 bars, as demonstrated in Figure 9.6, up to a lag of about 15 bars in one of the most stressing situations. This lag should be recognized when the measurement is used in trading.

Figure 9.9 shows the cycle period measurement of real data. This measurement is far more responsive than the more common measurements. Measurement accuracy can be tested by counting bars between major successive lowest lows or major successive highest highs and comparing the count to the measurement at that point. There are five bars per horizontal unit as a tip to help speed up your bar count. Please recall that there is about an eight-bar lag in the cycle measurement waveform.

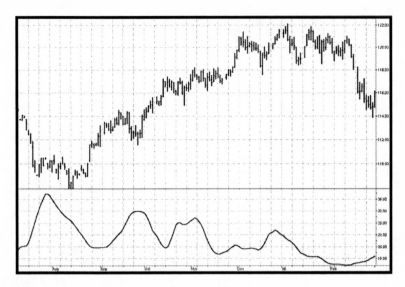

FIGURE 9.9 Cycle Measurement of Real Data

KEY POINTS TO REMEMBER

- The Hilbert transform enables the cycle period to be measured in as few as four bars.
- The cyclic component must be extracted from the data and then used to measure the Dominant Cycle period.
- The frequency discriminator to measure the Dominant Cycle period just sums the differential phases between bars until the sum reaches 360°—a full cycle.
- A five-bar median filter creates the differential phase to be summed.
- Summing the median differential phase enables the cycle measurement to be made using only five samples.
- The lag of measuring the Dominant Cycle period is about eight bars.
- The Dominant Cycle period measurement technique described in this chapter is the most responsive technique available.

CHAPTER 10

Adaptive Cycle Indicators

"The dinosaurs did not survive," said Tom adaptively.

Having made the cycle period measurements as in Chapter 9, one brute force application would be to note the most recent highest high and then count forward the number of bars equal to half the dominant cycle period to locate the next buying opportunity. Fortunately, we can be much more sophisticated in our analysis using indicators. If indicators work moderately well using fixed lengths in their computation, then these indicators should sparkle when the length is adaptive to a fraction of the measured dominant cycle.

I developed several oscillator-type indicators in Chapters 4 through 6. I will now revisit each of these and examine the improvements that result from using a Dominant Cycle measurement to make their computational length adaptive to the current market conditions. In each case, I compare the adaptive version of the indicator to the static version. I also compare the three adaptive indicators to each other for you to judge which is preferable. Since I use the same price chart throughout this book for consistency, and because you can test these indicators on your own computer using your own data, I will not bore you with agonizing details regarding indicator performance and comparisons.

ADAPTIVE CYBER CYCLE

The most simple cycle indicator was the Cyber Cycle, which was extracted from the price series in Chapter 4 by filtering out the trend component. The filter itself was derived in Chapter 2. This filter used the coefficient

$\alpha = 0.07$. The EasyLanguage and eSignal Formula Script (EFS) codes for the adaptive version of the Cyber Cycle Indicator are shown in Figures 10.1 and 10.2, respectively. Here, the Dominant Cycle is computed exactly as in Chapter 9. A fixed value of alpha is used to make the Dominant Cycle period measurement; then the measured Dominant Cycle is used to compute the coefficient alpha1. It is commonly recognized that the exponential moving alpha is related to the length of a simple moving average by the equation $\alpha = 2/(\text{Length} + 1)$. In this case, I use the Dominant Cycle period as the length in the computation of alpha1. This enables the Cyber Cycle Indicator to be adaptive to the measured Dominant Cycle period. A trigger signal consisting of the adaptive cycle delayed by one bar is also included in the indicator. Crossings of the adaptive cycle indicator and the trigger signal represent the buy and sell opportunities identified by this indicator.

Figure 10.3 shows the Adaptive Cyber Cycle Indicator compared to the static Cyber Cycle. This comparison shows that the adaptive indicator generally emphasizes the cyclic swings and is often one bar earlier in producing buy and sell signals.

ADAPTIVE CG INDICATOR

The CG Oscillator, derived in Chapter 5, finds the center of gravity of a fixed-length data sample as the sampling window is moved from bar to bar. The Adaptive CG Indicator uses half the measured Dominant Cycle period as the adaptive length of this variant of the CG Oscillator. The EasyLanguage and EFS codes for the adaptive version of the CG Oscillator are shown in Figures 10.4 and 10.5, respectively. Here, the dominant cycle is computed exactly as in Chapter 9. A fixed value of alpha is used to make the dominant cycle period measurement. The variable IntPeriod is computed as the integer portion of a four-bar weighted moving average of the Period. Since the weighted coefficients are divided by twice their sum, IntPeriod is the integer value of half the Dominant Cycle period. An integer value is required to sum the numerator and denominator in the subsequent code. Since the length of the summing varies with the length of the measured Dominant Cycle period, the CG is adaptive to it.

Figure 10.6 shows the Adaptive CG Indicator compared to the static CG Oscillator. This comparison in this data set does not display any dramatic change in the indicator as a result of making it adaptive.

ADAPTIVE RELATIVE VIGOR INDEX

The RVI, derived in Chapter 6, finds the difference of the close minus the open, normalized to the difference of the high and low. This ratio was

```
{***********************************************************
                    Adaptive Cycle
***********************************************************}
Inputs: Price((H+L)/2),
        alpha(.07);

Vars:   Smooth(0),
        Cycle(0),
        Q1(0),
        I1(0),
        DeltaPhase(0),
        MedianDelta(0),
        DC(0),
        InstPeriod(0),
        Period(0),
        Length(0),
        Num(0),
        Denom(0),
        alpha1(0),
        AdaptCycle(0);

Smooth = (Price + 2*Price[1] + 2*Price[2]
    + Price[3])/6;
Cycle = (1 - .5*alpha)*(1 - .5*alpha)*(Smooth
    - 2*Smooth[1] + Smooth[2]) + 2*(1 - alpha)*Cycle[1]
    - (1 - alpha)*(1 - alpha)*Cycle[2];
If currentbar < 7 then Cycle = (Price - 2*Price[1]
    + Price[2]) / 4;

Q1 = (.0962*Cycle + .5769*Cycle[2] - .5769*Cycle[4]
    - .0962*Cycle[6])*(.5 + .08*InstPeriod[1]);
I1 = Cycle[3];

If Q1 <> 0 and Q1[1] <> 0 then DeltaPhase = (I1/Q1
    - I1[1]/Q1[1]) / (1 + I1*I1[1]/(Q1*Q1[1]));
If DeltaPhase < 0.1 then DeltaPhase = 0.1;
If DeltaPhase > 1.1 then DeltaPhase = 1.1;
MedianDelta = Median(DeltaPhase, 5);

If MedianDelta = 0 then DC = 15 else DC = 6.28318
    / MedianDelta + .5;

InstPeriod = .33*DC + .67*InstPeriod[1];
```
                                          (continued)

FIGURE 10.1   EasyLanguage Code for the Adaptive Cyber Cycle

```
Period = .15*InstPeriod + .85*Period[1];

alpha1 = 2 / (Period + 1);
AdaptCycle = (1 - .5*alpha1)*(1 - .5*alpha1)*(Smooth
    - 2*Smooth[1] + Smooth[2]) + 2*(1
    - alpha1)*AdaptCycle[1] - (1 - alpha1)*(1
    - alpha1)*AdaptCycle[2];
If currentbar < 7 then AdaptCycle = (Price
    - 2*Price[1] + Price[2]) / 4;

Plot1(AdaptCycle, "AdaptCycle");
Plot2(AdaptCycle[1], "Trigger");
```

FIGURE 10.1   *(Continued)*

```
/*******************************************************
Title:       Adaptive Cyber Cycle Indicator
Coded By:  Chris D. Kryza (Divergence Software, Inc.)
Email:  c.kryza@gte.net
Incept:  07/09/2003
Version:  1.0.0


=========================================================
Fix History:

07/09/2003 -   Initial Release
1.0.0

=========================================================
*******************************************************/


//External Variables

var nBarCount              = 0;

var aPriceArray            = new Array();
var aSmoothArray           = new Array();
```

FIGURE 10.2   EFS Code for the Adaptive Cyber Cycle

```
var aCycleArray            = new Array();
var aDeltaPhase            = new Array();
var aPeriod                = new Array();
var aInstPeriod            = new Array();
var aQ1                    = new Array();
var aI1                    = new Array();
var aACycleArray           = new Array();

//== PreMain function required by eSignal to set_
    things up
function preMain() {
var x;

  setPriceStudy(false);
  setStudyTitle("Adaptive CyberCycle");
  setCursorLabelName("Cycle", 0);
  setCursorLabelName("Trig", 1);
  setDefaultBarFgColor( Color.blue, 0 );
  setDefaultBarFgColor( Color.red,  1 );

      //initialize arrays
  for (x=0; x<10; x++) {
      aPriceArray[x]        = 0.0;
      aSmoothArray[x]       = 0.0;
      aCycleArray[x]        = 0.0;
      aQ1[x]                = 0.0;
      aI1[x]                = 0.0;
      aDeltaPhase[x]        = 0.0;
      aPeriod[x]            = 0.0;
      aInstPeriod[x]        = 0.0;
      aACycleArray[x]       = 0.0;
  }


}

//== Main processing function
function main( Alpha ) {
var x;
var Alpha1;
var nDC;
var nMedianDelta;

      //initialize parameters if necessary
                                          (continued)
```

FIGURE 10.2 *(Continued)*

```
      if ( Alpha == null ) {
          Alpha = 0.07;
      }

      // study is initializing
  if (getBarState() == BARSTATE_ALLBARS) {
       return null;
  }

      //on each new bar, save array values
      if ( getBarState() == BARSTATE_NEWBAR ) {

          nBarCount++;

          aPriceArray.pop();
          aPriceArray.unshift( 0 );

          aSmoothArray.pop();
          aSmoothArray.unshift( 0 );

          aCycleArray.pop();
          aCycleArray.unshift( 0 );

          aQ1.pop();
          aQ1.unshift( 0 );

          aI1.pop();
          aI1.unshift( 0 );

          aDeltaPhase.pop();
          aDeltaPhase.unshift( 0 );

          aInstPeriod.pop();
          aInstPeriod.unshift( 0 );

          aPeriod.pop();
          aPeriod.unshift( 0 );

          aACycleArray.pop();
          aACycleArray.unshift( 0 );
```

FIGURE 10.2   *(Continued)*

```
      }

      aPriceArray[0] = ( high()+low() ) / 2;

      aSmoothArray[0] = ( aPriceArray[0]
          + 2*aPriceArray[1] + 2*aPriceArray[2]
          + aPriceArray[3] ) / 6;

      if ( nBarCount < 7 ) {
              aCycleArray[0] = ( aPriceArray[0]
                  - 2*aPriceArray[1] + aPriceArray[2] )
                  / 4;
      }
      else {
              aCycleArray[0] = ( 1 - 0.5*Alpha )
                  * ( 1 - 0.5*Alpha )
                  * ( aSmoothArray[0]
                  - 2*aSmoothArray[1]
                  + aSmoothArray[2] ) + 2*( 1-Alpha )
                  * aCycleArray[1] - ( 1-Alpha )
                  * ( 1-Alpha ) * aCycleArray[2];
      }

      aQ1[0] = ( 0.0962*aCycleArray[0]
          + 0.5769*aCycleArray[2]
          - 0.5769*aCycleArray[4]
          - 0.0962*aCycleArray[6] ) * ( 0.5 + 0.08
          * aInstPeriod[1] );
      aI1[0] = aCycleArray[3];

      if ( aQ1[0] != 0 && aQ1[1] != 0 ) {
              aDeltaPhase[0] = (aI1[0]/aQ1[0]
                  - aI1[1]/aQ1[1]) / (1
                  + aI1[0]*aI1[1]/(aQ1[0]*aQ1[1]));
      }
      if ( aDeltaPhase[0] < 0.1 ) aDeltaPhase[0]
          = 0.1;
      if ( aDeltaPhase[0] > 1.1 ) aDeltaPhase[0]
          = 1.1;

      nMedianDelta = Median( 5, aDeltaPhase );
                                      (continued)
```

FIGURE 10.2   *(Continued)*

```
      if ( nMedianDelta == 0 ) {
           nDC = 15;
      }
      else {
           nDC = 6.28318 / nMedianDelta + 0.5;
      }

      aInstPeriod[0] = 0.33 * nDC + 0.67
         * aInstPeriod[1];
      aPeriod[0] = 0.15*aInstPeriod[0]
         + 0.85*aPeriod[1];


      Alpha1 = 2 / ( aPeriod[0] + 1 );


      if ( nBarCount < 7 ) {
           aACycleArray[0] = (aPriceArray[0]
              - 2*aPriceArray[1]
              + aPriceArray[2])/4;
      }
      else {
           aACycleArray[0] = ( 1 - 0.5*Alpha1 )
              * ( 1 - 0.5*Alpha1 )
              * ( aSmoothArray[0]
              - 2*aSmoothArray[1] +
             aSmoothArray[2] ) + 2*( 1
                - Alpha1 ) * aACycleArray[1]
                - ( 1-Alpha1 ) * ( 1-Alpha1 )
                * aACycleArray[2];
      }


      //return the calculated values
      if (!isNaN( aACycleArray[0] ) ) {
           return new Array( aACycleArray[0],_
              aACycleArray[1] );
      }


  }
```

FIGURE 10.2   *(Continued)*

```
function Median( nBars, aArray ) {
var aTmp = new Array();
var nTmp;
var result;
var x;

        //transfer elements to temp array
        x = 0;
        while( x < nBars ) {
                aTmp[x] = aArray[x++];
        }
        //sort array in asc order
        aTmp.sort( SortAsc );


        //if odd # of elements, just take middle
        if ( nBars % 2 != 0 ) {
                result = aTmp[ (nBars+1) / 2 ]
                aTmp = null;
                return( result );
        }
        //if even # elements, take average of two middle
            elements
        else {
                nTmp = nBars/2;
                result = (aTmp[nTmp] + aTmp[nTmp+1])/2;
                aTmp = null;
                return ( result );
        }
}


function SortAsc( arg1, arg2 ) {
    if (arg1<arg2) {
      return( -1 )
    }
    else {
      return( 1 );
    }
}
```

FIGURE 10.2 *(Continued)*

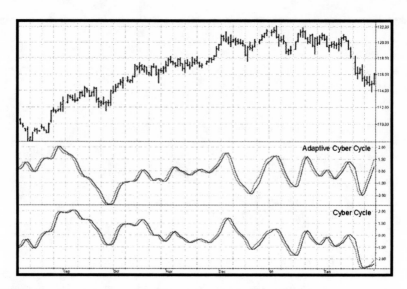

FIGURE 10.3 Adaptive Cyber Cycle Indicator Is More Responsive to Cyclic Price Variations than Static Cyber Cycle Indicator

```
{***********************************************************
                         Adaptive CG
************************************************************}
Inputs: Price((H+L)/2),
        alpha(.07);

Vars:   Smooth(0),
        Cycle(0),
        Q1(0),
        I1(0),
        DeltaPhase(0),
        MedianDelta(0),
        DC(0),
        InstPeriod(0),
        Period(0),
        count(0),
        Num(0),
        Denom(0),
        CG(0),
        IntPeriod(0);
```

FIGURE 10.4 EasyLanguage Code to Compute the Adaptive CG Indicator

```
Smooth = (Price + 2*Price[1] + 2*Price[2]
    + Price[3])/6;
Cycle = (1 - .5*alpha)*(1 - .5*alpha)*(Smooth
    - 2*Smooth[1] + Smooth[2]) + 2*(1 - alpha)*Cycle[1]
    - (1 - alpha)*(1 - alpha)*Cycle[2];
If currentbar < 7 then Cycle = (Price - 2*Price[1]
    + Price[2]) / 4;

Q1 = (.0962*Cycle + .5769*Cycle[2] - .5769*Cycle[4]
    - .0962*Cycle[6])*(.5 + .08*InstPeriod[1]);
I1 = Cycle[3];

If Q1 <> 0 and Q1[1] <> 0 then DeltaPhase = (I1/Q1
    - I1[1]/Q1[1]) / (1 + I1*I1[1]/(Q1*Q1[1]));
If DeltaPhase < 0.1 then DeltaPhase = 0.1;
If DeltaPhase > 1.1 then DeltaPhase = 1.1;
MedianDelta = Median(DeltaPhase, 5);

If MedianDelta = 0 then DC = 15 else DC = 6.28318
    / MedianDelta + .5;

InstPeriod = .33*DC + .67*InstPeriod[1];
Value1 = .15*InstPeriod + .85*Value1[1];
IntPeriod = intportion(Value1 / 2);

Num = 0;
Denom = 0;
For count = 0 to IntPeriod - 1 begin
        Num = Num + (1 + count)*(Price[count]);
        Denom = Denom + (Price[count]);
End;
If Denom <> 0 then CG = -Num/Denom + (IntPeriod + 1)
    / 2;

Plot1(CG, "CG");
Plot2(CG[1], "Trigger");
```

FIGURE 10.4 *(Continued)*

```
/**********************************************************
Title:       Adaptive CG Oscillator
Coded By:  Chris D. Kryza (Divergence Software, Inc.)
Email:  c.kryza@gte.net
Incept:  07/09/2003
Version:  1.0.0



===========================================================
Fix History:

07/09/2003 -    Initial Release
1.0.0


===========================================================
**********************************************************/


//External Variables

var nBarCount              = 0;

var aPriceArray            = new Array();
var aSmoothArray           = new Array();
var aCycleArray            = new Array();
var aDeltaPhase            = new Array();
var aPeriod                = new Array();
var aInstPeriod            = new Array();
var aQ1                    = new Array();
var aI1                    = new Array();
var aCGArray               = new Array();



//== PreMain function required by eSignal to set_
   things up
function preMain() {
var x;

  setPriceStudy(false);
  setStudyTitle("Adaptive CG");
  setCursorLabelName("CG", 0);
```

FIGURE 10.5   EFS Code to Compute the Adaptive CG Indicator

```
    setCursorLabelName("Trig", 1);
    setDefaultBarFgColor( Color.blue, 0 );
    setDefaultBarFgColor( Color.red,  1 );

        //initialize arrays
    for (x=0; x<70; x++) {
        aPriceArray[x]      = 0.0;
        aSmoothArray[x]     = 0.0;
        aCycleArray[x]      = 0.0;
        aQ1[x]              = 0.0;
        aI1[x]              = 0.0;
        aDeltaPhase[x]      = 0.0;
        aPeriod[x]          = 0.0;
        aInstPeriod[x]      = 0.0;
        aCGArray[x]         = 0.0;
    }

}

//== Main processing function
function main( Alpha ) {
var x;
var nCG = 0;
var nDC;
var nIntPeriod;
var nNum;
var nDenom;
var nMedianDelta;

        //initialize parameters if necessary
        if ( Alpha == null ) {
              Alpha = 0.07;
        }

        // study is initializing
    if (getBarState() == BARSTATE_ALLBARS) {
      return null;
    }

        //on each new bar, save array values
        if ( getBarState() == BARSTATE_NEWBAR ) {
                                                  (continued)
```

FIGURE 10.5 *(Continued)*

```
            nBarCount++;

            aPriceArray.pop();
            aPriceArray.unshift( 0 );

            aSmoothArray.pop();
            aSmoothArray.unshift( 0 );

            aCycleArray.pop();
            aCycleArray.unshift( 0 );

            aQ1.pop();
            aQ1.unshift( 0 );

            aI1.pop();
            aI1.unshift( 0 );

            aDeltaPhase.pop();
            aDeltaPhase.unshift( 0 );

            aInstPeriod.pop();
            aInstPeriod.unshift( 0 );

            aPeriod.pop();
            aPeriod.unshift( 0 );

            aCGArray.pop();
            aCGArray.unshift( 0 );


    }

    aPriceArray[0] = ( high()+low() ) / 2;

    aSmoothArray[0] = ( aPriceArray[0]
        + 2*aPriceArray[1] + 2*aPriceArray[2]
        + aPriceArray[3] ) / 6;

    if ( nBarCount < 7 ) {
            aCycleArray[0] = ( aPriceArray[0]
                - 2*aPriceArray[1]
                + aPriceArray[2] ) / 4;
```

FIGURE 10.5   *(Continued)*

```
    }
    else {
        aCycleArray[0] = ( 1 - 0.5*Alpha ) * ( 1
            - 0.5*Alpha ) * ( aSmoothArray[0]
            - 2*aSmoothArray[1]
            + aSmoothArray[2] ) + 2*( 1-Alpha )
            * aCycleArray[1] - ( 1-Alpha ) * ( 1-
            Alpha ) * aCycleArray[2];
    }

    aQ1[0] = ( 0.0962*aCycleArray[0]
        + 0.5769*aCycleArray[2]
        - 0.5769*aCycleArray[4]
        - 0.0962*aCycleArray[6] ) * ( 0.5 + 0.08
        * aInstPeriod[1] );
    aI1[0] = aCycleArray[3];

    if ( aQ1[0] != 0 && aQ1[1] != 0 ) {
        aDeltaPhase[0] = (aI1[0]/aQ1[0]
            - aI1[1]/aQ1[1]) / (1
            + aI1[0]*aI1[1]/(aQ1[0]*aQ1[1]));
    }
    if ( aDeltaPhase[0] < 0.1 ) aDeltaPhase[0]
        = 0.1;
    if ( aDeltaPhase[0] > 1.1 ) aDeltaPhase[0]
        = 1.1;

    nMedianDelta = Median( 5, aDeltaPhase );

    if ( nMedianDelta == 0 ) {
        nDC = 15;
    }
    else {
        nDC = 6.28318 / nMedianDelta + 0.5;
    }

    aInstPeriod[0] = 0.33 * nDC + 0.67
        * aInstPeriod[1];
    aPeriod[0] = 0.15*aInstPeriod[0]
        + 0.85*aPeriod[1];
```

(continued)

FIGURE 10.5   *(Continued)*

```
nIntPeriod = Math.floor( ( 4*aPeriod[0]
    + 3*aPeriod[1] +
    2*aPeriod[3] + aPeriod[4] ) / 20 );

nNum            = 0;
nDenom          = 0;


for ( x=0; x<nIntPeriod; x++ ){
    nNum += ( 1.0 + x )
        * ( aPriceArray[x]  );
    nDenom += ( aPriceArray[x] );
}


if ( nDenom != 0 ) nCG = -nNum/nDenom
    + ( nIntPeriod+1 )/2;
aCGArray[0] = nCG;


//return the calculated values
if (!isNaN( aCGArray[0] ) ) {
    return new Array( aCGArray[0],
        aCGArray[1] );
}


}



function Median( nBars, aArray ) {
var aTmp = new Array();
var nTmp;
var result;
var x;

    //transfer elements to temp array
    x = 0;
    while( x < nBars ) {
        aTmp[x] = aArray[x++];
```

FIGURE 10.5 *(Continued)*

```
        }
        //sort array in asc order
        aTmp.sort( SortAsc );


        //if odd # of elements, just take middle
        if ( nBars % 2 != 0 ) {
                result = aTmp[ (nBars+1) / 2 ]
                aTmp = null;
                return( result );
        }
        //if even # elements, take average of two middle_
            elements
        else {
                nTmp = nBars/2;
                result = (aTmp[nTmp] + aTmp[nTmp+1])/2;
                aTmp = null;
                return ( result );
        }
}


function SortAsc( arg1, arg2 ) {
        if (arg1<arg2) {
            return( -1 )
        }
        else {
            return( 1 );
        }
}
```

FIGURE 10.5   *(Continued)*

computed over a fixed period. The Adaptive RVI Indicator uses half the measured Dominant Cycle period as the adaptive length of this variant of the RVI. The EasyLanguage and EFS codes for the adaptive version of the RVI are shown in Figures 10.7 and 10.8, respectively. Here the Dominant Cycle is computed exactly as in Chapter 9. A fixed value of alpha is used to make the Dominant Cycle period measurement. The variable Length is computed as the integer portion of a four-bar weighted moving average of the period. Since the weighted coefficients are divided by twice their sum,

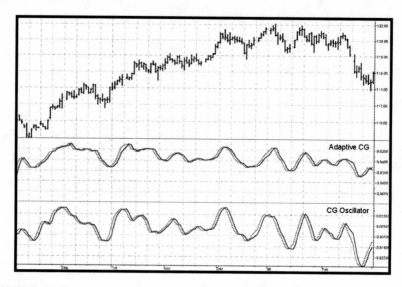

FIGURE 10.6 Adaptive CG Indicator Compared to Static CG Oscillator

```
{******************************************************
                    Adaptive RVI
******************************************************}
Inputs: Price((H+L)/2),
        alpha(.07);

Vars:   Smooth(0),
        Cycle(0),
        Q1(0),
        I1(0),
        DeltaPhase(0),
        MedianDelta(0),
        DC(0),
        InstPeriod(0),
        Period(0),
        count(0),
        Length(0),
        Num(0),
        Denom(0),
        RVI(0),
        MaxRVI(0),
```

FIGURE 10.7 EasyLanguage Code to Compute the Adaptive RVI

```
         MinRVI(0);
Smooth = (Price + 2*Price[1] + 2*Price[2]
   + Price[3])/6;
Cycle = (1 - .5*alpha)*(1 - .5*alpha)*(Smooth
   - 2*Smooth[1] + Smooth[2]) + 2*(1 - alpha)*Cycle[1]
   - (1 - alpha)*(1 - alpha)*Cycle[2];
If currentbar < 7 then Cycle = (Price - 2*Price[1]
   + Price[2]) / 4;

Q1 = (.0962*Cycle + .5769*Cycle[2] - .5769*Cycle[4]
   - .0962*Cycle[6])*(.5 + .08*InstPeriod[1]);
I1 = Cycle[3];

If Q1 <> 0 and Q1[1] <> 0 then DeltaPhase = (I1/Q1
   - I1[1]/Q1[1]) / (1 + I1*I1[1]/(Q1*Q1[1]));
If DeltaPhase < 0.1 then DeltaPhase = 0.1;
If DeltaPhase > 1.1 then DeltaPhase = 1.1;
MedianDelta = Median(DeltaPhase, 5);

If MedianDelta = 0 then DC = 15 else DC = 6.28318
   / MedianDelta + .5;

InstPeriod = .33*DC + .67*InstPeriod[1];
Period = .15*InstPeriod + .85*Period[1];
Length = intportion((4*Period + 3*Period[1]
   + 2*Period[3] + Period[4]) / 20);

Value1 = ((Close - Open) + 2*(Close[1] - Open[1])
   + 2*(Close[2] - Open[2]) + (Close[3] - Open[3]))/6;
Value2 = ((High - Low) + 2*(High[1] - Low[1])
   + 2*(High[2] - Low[2]) + (High[3] - Low[3]))/6;
Num = 0;
Denom = 0;
For count = 0 to Length - 1 begin
      Num = Num + Value1[count];
      Denom = Denom + Value2[count];
End;
If Denom <> 0 then RVI = Num / Denom;

Plot1(RVI, "RVI");
Plot2(RVI[1], "Trigger");
```

FIGURE 10.7 *(Continued)*

```
/**********************************************************
Title:        Adaptive RVI
Coded By:  Chris D. Kryza (Divergence Software, Inc.)
Email:  c.kryza@gte.net
Incept:  07/09/2003
Version:  1.0.0



==========================================================
Fix History:

07/09/2003 -    Initial Release
1.0.0


==========================================================
**********************************************************/


//External Variables

var nBarCount            = 0;

var aPriceArray          = new Array();
var aSmoothArray         = new Array();
var aCycleArray          = new Array();
var aDeltaPhase          = new Array();
var aPeriod              = new Array();
var aInstPeriod          = new Array();
var aQ1                  = new Array();
var aI1                  = new Array();
var aRVIArray            = new Array();
var aV1Array             = new Array();
var aV2Array             = new Array();


//== PreMain function required by eSignal to set_
    things up
function preMain() {
var x;

  setPriceStudy(false);
  setStudyTitle("Adaptive RVI");
```

FIGURE 10.8   EFS Code to Compute the Adaptive RVI

```
setCursorLabelName("RVI", 0);
setCursorLabelName("Trig", 1);
setDefaultBarFgColor( Color.blue, 0 );
setDefaultBarFgColor( Color.red,  1 );

    //initialize arrays
for (x=0; x<70; x++) {
    aPriceArray[x]      = 0.0;
    aSmoothArray[x]     = 0.0;
    aCycleArray[x]      = 0.0;
    aQ1[x]              = 0.0;
    aI1[x]              = 0.0;
    aDeltaPhase[x]      = 0.0;
    aPeriod[x]          = 0.0;
    aInstPeriod[x]      = 0.0;
    aRVIArray[x]        = 0.0;
    aV1Array[x]         = 0.0;
    aV2Array[x]         = 0.0;
}

}

//== Main processing function
function main( Alpha ) {
var x;
var nRVI = 0;
var nDC;
var nLength;
var nNum;
var nDenom;
var nMedianDelta;

    //initialize parameters if necessary
    if ( Alpha == null ) {
        Alpha = 0.07;
    }

    // study is initializing
  if (getBarState() == BARSTATE_ALLBARS) {
    return null;
  }
```

(continued)

FIGURE 10.8 *(Continued)*

```
        //on each new bar, save array values
        if ( getBarState() == BARSTATE_NEWBAR ) {

                nBarCount++;

                aPriceArray.pop();
                aPriceArray.unshift( 0 );

                aSmoothArray.pop();
                aSmoothArray.unshift( 0 );

                aCycleArray.pop();
                aCycleArray.unshift( 0 );

                aQ1.pop();
                aQ1.unshift( 0 );

                aI1.pop();
                aI1.unshift( 0 );

                aDeltaPhase.pop();
                aDeltaPhase.unshift( 0 );

                aInstPeriod.pop();
                aInstPeriod.unshift( 0 );

                aPeriod.pop();
                aPeriod.unshift( 0 );

                aRVIArray.pop();
                aRVIArray.unshift( 0 );

                aV1Array.pop();
                aV1Array.unshift( 0 );

                aV2Array.pop();
                aV2Array.unshift( 0 );

        }

        aPriceArray[0] = ( high()+low() ) / 2;
```

FIGURE 10.8 *(Continued)*

```
aSmoothArray[0] = ( aPriceArray[0]
    + 2*aPriceArray[1] + 2*aPriceArray[2]
    + aPriceArray[3] ) / 6;

if ( nBarCount < 7 ) {
    aCycleArray[0] = ( aPriceArray[0]
        - 2*aPriceArray[1] + aPriceArray[2] )
        / 4;
}
else {
    aCycleArray[0] = ( 1 - 0.5*Alpha ) * ( 1
        - 0.5*Alpha ) * ( aSmoothArray[0]
        - 2*aSmoothArray[1]
        + aSmoothArray[2] ) + 2*( 1-Alpha )
        * aCycleArray[1] - ( 1-Alpha ) * ( 1-
        Alpha ) * aCycleArray[2];
}

aQ1[0] = ( 0.0962*aCycleArray[0]
    + 0.5769*aCycleArray[2]
    - 0.5769*aCycleArray[4]
    - 0.0962*aCycleArray[6] ) * ( 0.5 + 0.08
    * aInstPeriod[1] );
aI1[0] = aCycleArray[3];

if ( aQ1[0] != 0 && aQ1[1] != 0 ) {
    aDeltaPhase[0] = (aI1[0]/aQ1[0]
        - aI1[1]/aQ1[1])
        / (1 + aI1[0]*aI1[1]/(aQ1[0]*aQ1[1]));
}
if ( aDeltaPhase[0] < 0.1 ) aDeltaPhase[0]
    = 0.1;
if ( aDeltaPhase[0] > 1.1 ) aDeltaPhase[0]
    = 1.1;

nMedianDelta = Median( 5, aDeltaPhase );

nPhaseSum           = 0;
nOldPhaseSum        = 0;
nDC                 = 0;

if ( nMedianDelta == 0 ) {
                                    (continued)
```

FIGURE 10.8 *(Continued)*

```
        nDC = 15;
}
else {
      nDC = 6.28318 / nMedianDelta + 0.5;
}

aInstPeriod[0] = 0.33 * nDC + 0.67
    * aInstPeriod[1];
aPeriod[0] = 0.15*aInstPeriod[0]
    + 0.85*aPeriod[1];

nLength = Math.floor( ( 4*aPeriod[0]
    + 3*aPeriod[1] +
            2*aPeriod[3] + aPeriod[4] ) / 20 );

aV1Array[0] = ( ( close()-open() )
    + 2*( close(-1)-open(-1) )
    + 2*( close(-2)-open(-2) )
    + ( close(-3)-open(-3) ) ) / 6;
aV2Array[0] = ( ( high()-low() )
    + 2*( high(-1)-low(-1) )
    + 2*( high(-2)-low(-2) )
    + ( high(-3)-low(-3) ) ) / 6;

nNum            = 0;
nDenom          = 0;

for ( x=0; x<nLength; x++ ){
      nNum += aV1Array[x];
      nDenom += aV2Array[x];
}


if ( nDenom != 0 ) nRVI = nNum/nDenom;
aRVIArray[0] = nRVI;


//return the calculated values
if (!isNaN( aRVIArray[0] ) ) {
      return new Array( aRVIArray[0],_
          aRVIArray[1] );
}
```

FIGURE 10.8   *(Continued)*

```
}

function Median( nBars, aArray ) {
var aTmp = new Array();
var nTmp;
var result;
var x;

        //transfer elements to temp array
        x = 0;
        while( x < nBars ) {
                aTmp[x] = aArray[x++];
        }
        //sort array in asc order
        aTmp.sort( SortAsc );


        //if odd # of elements, just take middle
        if ( nBars % 2 != 0 ) {
                result = aTmp[ (nBars+1) / 2 ]
                aTmp = null;
                return( result );
        }
        //if even # elements, take average of two middle
           elements
        else {
                nTmp = nBars/2;
                result = (aTmp[nTmp] + aTmp[nTmp+1])/2;
                aTmp = null;
                return ( result );
        }
}


function SortAsc( arg1, arg2 ) {
      if (arg1<arg2) {
         return( -1 )
      }
      else {
           return( 1 );
      }
}
```

FIGURE 10.8 *(Continued)*

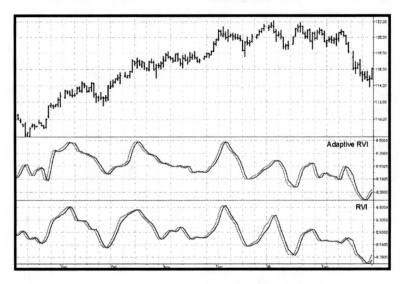

FIGURE 10.9 The Adaptive RVI Is More Responsive to Shorter Cycle Variations than the Static RVI

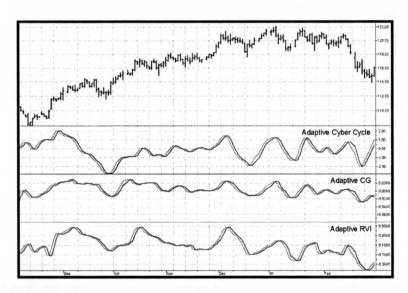

FIGURE 10.10 Adaptive Indicator Comparison

Length is the integer value of half the Dominant Cycle period. An integer value is required to sum the numerator and denominator in the subsequent code. Since the length of the summing varies with the length of the measured Dominant Cycle period, the RVI is adaptive to it.

Figure 10.9 shows the Adaptive RVI compared to the static RVI. As with the other adaptive indicators, the contributions of the shorter cycle periods are emphasized when compared to their static variants.

Figure 10.10 shows the three adaptive indicators compared to each other. As with their static variants, all show about the same performance. Perhaps the message is that once the cyclic component is extracted from the data correctly, most oscillator-type indicators have about the same performance. It may be true that one indicator performs better in one data set than another. The bottom line is that you now have in your toolbox three independently derived indicators from which to choose. It then becomes a matter of personal preference.

KEY POINTS TO REMEMBER

- The adaptive indicators all use the measured Dominant Cycle as their adaptive criterion.
- The Adaptive Cyber Cycle adapts to the full Dominant Cycle period in the computation of its alpha1 filter parameter.
- The Adaptive CG Oscillator uses the integer portion of the half Dominant Cycle period in the computation of the filter center of gravity.
- The Adaptive RVI uses the integer portion of the half Dominant Cycle period in the computation of the vigor ratio.
- All three adaptive indicators demonstrate similar performance.

CHAPTER 11

The Sinewave Indicator

"I can forecast the future," said Tom predictably.

Causal filters can never predict the future. In fact, all have lag. The purpose of making good indicators adaptive in Chapter 9 was to eliminate as much lag as possible, not to make a prediction. With the Sinewave Indicator we are trying to create a noncausal filter that can predict the turning point of market cycles. Anticipation of the cyclic turning points is a major advantage of the Sinewave Indicator when compared to other oscillators, such as the RSI and Stochastic Indicators, that must wait for confirmation.

In Chapter 9 I showed you how to measure the period of the dominant market cycle for any bar in the data series. However, this measurement does not tell us where we are within that cycle. To locate the position of the cycle, we must measure the phase of the Dominant Cycle. Knowing the phase of the cycle, we can take the sine of the measured phase to create an artificial oscillator-type indicator. That is, the cyclic component of the market data is synthesized as a pure sinewave. Any lag we created in the process of measuring the phase can be mathematically removed. Furthermore, simply adding 45° to the measured phase creates an artificial phase lead. This is the noncausal factor. The phase is advanced on the presumption that the measured cycle has existed (at least briefly) in the past and will continue (at least briefly) into the future. Advancing the phase by 45° and taking a sine of the advanced phase angle produces an oscillator waveshape that leads the original sinewave by one-eighth of a cycle. The two sinewaves therefore cross ¹⁄₁₆ of a cycle before the peak cycle turning point and before the valley turning point. For a 16-bar Dominant Cycle, this gives an ideal 1-bar advance warning of the absolute Dominant Cycle turning points. For a 48-bar cycle, the advance extends to 3 bars. For an eight-bar Dominant Cycle, the advance warning is theoretically only half a bar.

My simplified model of the market consists of a trend and a cycle. There are certainly additional components present in real markets, but we are ignoring them in this simplified model. I call the highest-amplitude cycle the Dominant Cycle. Experience bears out that the assumption of the presence of a single Dominant Cycle is a workable approximation. Knowing the Dominant Cycle period, the phase of this Dominant Cycle can be measured. But if the market goes into a pure trend, there is no cycle. In this case, the phase ceases to advance. If the phase does not advance, then the two sinewave waveshapes of the Sinewave Indicator cannot cross. If the two waveshapes do not cross, the Sinewave Indicator produces no cyclic buy or sell signals. This avoidance of false whipsaw signals is a distinct advantage over traditional oscillators. In practice, the phase does not exactly stop; the phase does languish and the phase waveshape appears distinctly different than the constant rate of change that is produced when the market is in a cycle mode. The phase varies between 0° and 360°. If the cycle period is changing, there is an occasional crossing of the Sinewave Indicator lines to correct the phase angle for the current cycle period measurement. In these cases, the Sinewave Indicator lines do not appear to be sinewaves in the vicinity of the crossing. Therefore, these occasional bad crossing signals are easy to identify.

We obtain the Sinewave Indicator by plotting the sine of the measured phase angle. This gives us an oscillator that always swings between the limits of −1 and +1. We enhance the usability of this oscillator by plotting the sine of the phase angle advanced by 45°. The effect of plotting these two lines is shown for both the phasor and time domain presentations in Figure 11.1. Adding 45° clearly advances the phasor from a 45° slant to the vertical position. This phase advance means the LeadSine waveform will crest before the Sine crests. The LeadSine and Sine lines cross 22.5°, or ¹⁄₁₆ of a cycle, before the turning point of the cycle is reached. If the market has a cycle of 16 bars or less, this is a signal to enter or exit a trade immediately. If the market has a longer cycle, there is some built-in anticipation time before you pull the trigger.

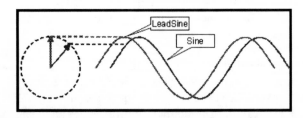

FIGURE 11.1　Phasor and Time Domain Views of the Sinewave Indicator

Compared to conventional oscillators such as the Stochastic or RSI, the Sinewave Indicator has two major advantages. These are as follows:

1. The Sinewave Indicator anticipates the Cycle Mode turning point rather than waiting for confirmation.
2. The phase does not advance when the market is in a Trend Mode. Therefore the Sinewave Indicator does not tend to give false whipsaw signals when the market is in a Trend Mode.

An additional advantage is that the anticipation signal is obtained strictly by mathematically advancing the phase. Momentum is not employed. Therefore, the Sinewave Indicator signals are no more noisy than the original signal.

The EasyLanguage and eSignal Formula Script (EFS) codes to measure Dominant Cycle phase and then to synthesize the Sinewave are described with reference to Figures 11.2 and 11.3, respectively. The initial part of the code measures the Dominant Cycle exactly as in Chapter 9. The measured period must be further smoothed using an exponential moving average ($\alpha = 0.15$) because there is no further smoothing in the computation of the phase. The variable DCPeriod is the integer portion of the smoothed Dominant Cycle period because it is used to sum over the period and only an integer variable can be used for this purpose. Otherwise, rounding errors cause erratic results. The cycle component of the data is multiplied individually with the sine and cosine of the Dominant Cycle period, and these two products are summed individually over one complete cycle. These sums are known as the real part and the imaginary part of the data. It is well known that the arctangent of their ratio is the phase of cycle component. The arctangent function can go to infinity, and the code precludes a computational problem if the ImagPart variable is smaller than 0.001. The arctangent function is also subject to ambiguities, depending on in which phase quadrant the computation resides. In EasyLanguage, it is simplest to resolve these ambiguities by rotating the DCPhase by 90° and then adding another 180° if ImagPart is negative. If converting this code to another language, care should be taken when dealing with the arctangent function. First, most computer languages represent angles in terms of radians rather than degrees. Second, the ambiguity resolution scheme I used is not universally appropriate for all languages. The Sine Indicator is plotted simply as the sine of the phase angle of the Dominant Cycle and the LeadSine Indicator is plotted as the sine of the phase angle plus 45°, giving it the desired leading property.

The Sinewave Indicators are plotted against both theoretical analytic waveforms and real-world data to demonstrate their performance. Figure 11.4 shows a theoretical 20-bar cycle sinewave analytic waveform. Note

```
{*********************************************************
                   Sinewave Indicator
 *********************************************************}

Inputs: Price((H+L)/2),
        alpha(.07);

Vars:   Smooth(0),
        Cycle(0),
        I1(0),
        Q1(0),
        I2(0),
        Q2(0),
        DeltaPhase(0),
        MedianDelta(0),
        MaxAmp(0),
        AmpFix(0),
        Re(0),
        Im(0),
        DC(0),
        alpha1(0),
        InstPeriod(0),
        DCPeriod(0),
        count(0),
        SmoothCycle(0),
        RealPart(0),
        ImagPart(0),
        DCPhase(0);

Smooth = (Price + 2*Price[1] + 2*Price[2]
    + Price[3])/6;
Cycle = (1 - .5*alpha)*(1 - .5*alpha)*(Smooth
    - 2*Smooth[1] + Smooth[2]) + 2*(1 - alpha)*Cycle[1]
    - (1 - alpha)*(1 - alpha)*Cycle[2];
If currentbar < 7 then Cycle = (Price - 2*Price[1]
    + Price[2]) / 4;
{Cycle = Price;}
Q1 = (.0962*Cycle + .5769*Cycle[2] - .5769*Cycle[4]
    - .0962*Cycle[6])*(.5 + .08*InstPeriod[1]);
I1 = Cycle[3];

If Q1 <> 0 and Q1[1] <> 0 then DeltaPhase = (I1/Q1
    - I1[1]/Q1[1]) / (1 + I1*I1[1]/(Q1*Q1[1]));
```

FIGURE 11.2 EasyLanguage Code to Compute the Sinewave Indicator

```
If DeltaPhase < 0.1 then DeltaPhase = 0.1;
If DeltaPhase > 1.1 then DeltaPhase = 1.1;
MedianDelta = Median(DeltaPhase, 5);

If MedianDelta = 0 then DC = 15 else DC = 6.28318 /
    MedianDelta + .5;

InstPeriod = .33*DC + .67*InstPeriod[1];
Value1 = .15*InstPeriod + .85*Value1[1];

{Compute Dominant Cycle Phase}
DCPeriod = IntPortion(Value1);
RealPart = 0;
ImagPart = 0;
For count = 0 To DCPeriod  - 1 begin
        RealPart = RealPart + Sine(360 * count
            / DCPeriod) * (Cycle[count]);
        ImagPart = ImagPart + Cosine(360 * count
            / DCPeriod) * (Cycle[count]);
End;
If AbsValue(ImagPart) > 0.001 then DCPhase
    = Arctangent(RealPart / ImagPart);
If AbsValue(ImagPart) <= 0.001 then DCPhase = 90
    * Sign(RealPart);

DCPhase = DCPhase + 90;
If ImagPart < 0 then DCPhase = DCPhase + 180;
If DCPhase > 315 then DCPhase = DCPhase - 360;

Plot1(Sine(DCPhase), "Sine");
Plot2(Sine(DCPhase + 45), "LeadSine");
```

FIGURE 11.2   *(Continued)*

how the LeadSine crosses over the Sine immediately prior to each peak and valley in the price waveform. The LeadSine always crosses the Sine line before the turning point in the cycle, giving advance indication of the cyclic turning point. The amount of advance warning relative to the length of the cycle is less for the shorter cycles.

The Sinewave Indicator is plotted in the bottom graph for the standard data set in Figure 11.5. The market is in a trend at the left side of the chart in August and September. We know this because the wiggles in the

```
/*******************************************************
Title:      Sine Wave Indicator
Coded By:  Chris D. Kryza (Divergence Software, Inc.)
Email:  c.kryza@gte.net
Incept:  07/09/2003
Version:  1.0.0



=========================================================
Fix History:

07/09/2003 -    Initial Release
1.0.0


=========================================================
*******************************************************/


//External Variables

var nBarCount           = 0;

var aPriceArray         = new Array();
var aSmoothArray        = new Array();
var aCycleArray         = new Array();
var aDeltaPhase         = new Array();
var aPeriod             = new Array();
var aInstPeriod         = new Array();
var aQ1                 = new Array();
var aI1                 = new Array();
var aV1Array            = new Array();

//== PreMain function required by eSignal to set_
   things up
function preMain() {
var x;

  setPriceStudy(false);
  setStudyTitle("Sine Wave");
  setCursorLabelName("Sine", 0);
  setCursorLabelName("LeadSine", 1);
  setDefaultBarFgColor( Color.blue, 0 );
```

FIGURE 11.3 EFS Code for the Sinewave Indicator

```
   setDefaultBarFgColor( Color.red,  1 );

      //initialize arrays
   for (x=0; x<70; x++) {
      aPriceArray[x]      = 0.0;
      aSmoothArray[x]     = 0.0;
      aCycleArray[x]      = 0.0;
      aQ1[x]              = 0.0;
      aI1[x]              = 0.0;
      aDeltaPhase[x]      = 0.0;
      aPeriod[x]          = 0.0;
      aInstPeriod[x]      = 0.0;
      aV1Array[x]         = 0.0;
   }


}

//== Main processing function
function main( Alpha ) {
var x;
var nDC;
var nDCPeriod;
var nRealPart;
var nImagPart;
var nDCPhase = 0.0;
var nMedianDelta;

      //initialize parameters if necessary
      if ( Alpha == null ) {
            Alpha = 0.07;
      }

      // study is initializing
   if (getBarState() == BARSTATE_ALLBARS) {
     return null;
   }

      //on each new bar, save array values
      if ( getBarState() == BARSTATE_NEWBAR ) {

            nBarCount++;

                                           (continued)
```

FIGURE 11.3   (Continued)

```
                aPriceArray.pop();
                aPriceArray.unshift( 0 );

                aSmoothArray.pop();
                aSmoothArray.unshift( 0 );

                aCycleArray.pop();
                aCycleArray.unshift( 0 );

                aQ1.pop();
                aQ1.unshift( 0 );

                aI1.pop();
                aI1.unshift( 0 );

                aDeltaPhase.pop();
                aDeltaPhase.unshift( 0 );

                aInstPeriod.pop();
                aInstPeriod.unshift( 0 );

                aPeriod.pop();
                aPeriod.unshift( 0 );

                aV1Array.pop();
                aV1Array.unshift( 0 );


        }

        aPriceArray[0] = ( high()+low() ) / 2;

        aSmoothArray[0] = ( aPriceArray[0]
            + 2*aPriceArray[1] + 2*aPriceArray[2]
            + aPriceArray[3] ) / 6;

        if ( nBarCount < 7 ) {
                aCycleArray[0] = ( aPriceArray[0]
                    - 2*aPriceArray[1] + aPriceArray[2] )
                    / 4;
        }
        else {
```

FIGURE 11.3 *(Continued)*

```
            aCycleArray[0] = ( 1 - 0.5*Alpha )
                * ( 1 - 0.5*Alpha )
                * ( aSmoothArray[0] - 2
                *aSmoothArray[1] + aSmoothArray[2] )
                + 2*( 1-Alpha ) * aCycleArray[1]
                - ( 1-Alpha ) * ( 1-Alpha )
                * aCycleArray[2];
    }

aQ1[0] = ( 0.0962*aCycleArray[0]
    + 0.5769*aCycleArray[2]
    - 0.5769*aCycleArray[4]
    - 0.0962*aCycleArray[6] ) * ( 0.5 + 0.08
    * aInstPeriod[1] );
aI1[0] = aCycleArray[3];

if ( aQ1[0] != 0 && aQ1[1] != 0 ) {
        aDeltaPhase[0] = (aI1[0]/aQ1[0]
            - aI1[1]/aQ1[1])
            / (1 + aI1[0]*aI1[1]/(aQ1[0]*aQ1[1]));
    }
if ( aDeltaPhase[0] < 0.1 ) aDeltaPhase[0]
    = 0.1;
if ( aDeltaPhase[0] > 1.1 ) aDeltaPhase[0]
    = 1.1;

nMedianDelta = Median( 5, aDeltaPhase );

if ( nMedianDelta == 0 ) {
        nDC = 15;
    }
else {
        nDC = 6.28318 / nMedianDelta + 0.5;
    }

aInstPeriod[0] = 0.33 * nDC + 0.67
    * aInstPeriod[1];
aPeriod[0] = 0.15*aInstPeriod[0]
    + 0.85*aPeriod[1];

aV1Array[0] = 0.15*aPeriod[0]
    + 0.85*aV1Array[1];
```

                                    (continued)

FIGURE 11.3   *(Continued)*

```
        //compute dominant cycle phase
        nDCPeriod = Math.floor( aV1Array[0] );
        nRealPart = 0.0;
        nImagPart = 0.0;

        for ( x=0; x<nDCPeriod; x++ ) {
              nRealPart += Math.sin( DegToRad_
                  ( 360*x/nDCPeriod ) )
                  * ( aCycleArray[x] );
              nImagPart += Math.cos( DegToRad_
                  ( 360*x/nDCPeriod ) )
                  * ( aCycleArray[x] );
        }

        if ( Math.abs( nImagPart ) > 0.001  ) nDCPhase
            =  RadToDeg( Math.atan_
            ( nRealPart/nImagPart ) );

        if ( Math.abs( nImagPart ) <= 0.001 ) nDCPhase
            = 90 * ( nRealPart<0 ? -1 : 1 );

        nDCPhase += 90;
        if ( nImagPart < 0 ) nDCPhase += 180;


        //return the calculated values
        if (!isNaN( nDCPhase ) ) {
              return new Array( Math.sin( DegToRad_
                  ( nDCPhase) ), Math.sin( DegToRad_
                  ( nDCPhase+45 ) ) );
        }


}


//== Convert Degrees to Radians
function DegToRad( nValue ) {
var nTmp;
      nTmp = nValue * ( Math.PI / 180 );
      return( nTmp );
}
```

FIGURE 11.3   *(Continued)*

```
//== Convert Radians to Degrees
function RadToDeg( nValue ) {
var nTmp;

        nTmp = nValue * ( 180 / Math.PI );

        return( nTmp );

}

function Median( nBars, aArray ) {
var aTmp = new Array();
var nTmp;
var result;
var x;

        //transfer elements to temp array
        x = 0;
        while( x < nBars ) {
                aTmp[x] = aArray[x++];
        }
        //sort array in asc order
        aTmp.sort( SortAsc );


        //if odd # of elements, just take middle
        if ( nBars % 2 != 0 ) {
                result = aTmp[ (nBars+1) / 2 ]
                aTmp = null;
                return( result );
        }
        //if even # elements, take average of two_
           middle elements
        else {
                nTmp = nBars/2;
                result = (aTmp[nTmp] + aTmp[nTmp+1])/2;
                aTmp = null;
                return ( result );
        }
}
```

(continued)

FIGURE 11.3 *(Continued)*

```
function SortAsc( arg1, arg2 ) {
      if (arg1<arg2) {
        return( -1 )
      }
      else {
        return( 1 );
      }
}
```

FIGURE 11.3 *(Continued)*

Sinewave Indicator do not cross. In other words, the Sinewave Indicator indicates that some kind of trend-following system should be used. Then there are three clear cyclic turning points until the trend is indicated again in November. This is a case where the phase is unwinding and there is no clear cyclic crossover in the indicator. The Sinewave Indicator then has six successive sterling turning points identified until the trend returns at the right side of the chart, near the end of February.

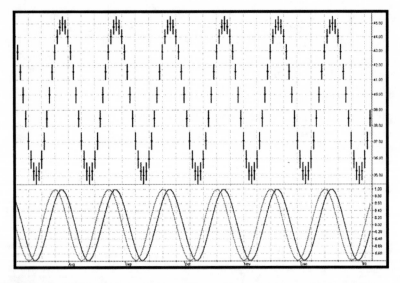

FIGURE 11.4 The Sinewave Indicator Always Gives an Advanced Turning Point Warning

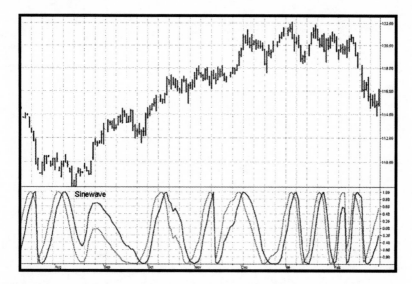

FIGURE 11.5 The Sinewave Indicator Gives Correct Cycle Signals

KEY POINTS TO REMEMBER

- The Sinewave Indicator is a noncausal predictive filter based on the premise that the Dominant Cycle has existed in the immediate past and will continue into the immediate future.
- The phase has a constant rate of change when the market is in a Cycle Mode.
- The phase languishes when the market is in a Trend Mode, and can even have a negative rate of change.
- The Sinewave Indicator consists of the sine of the Dominant Cycle phase and the sine of the Dominant Cycle phase advanced by 45°.
- The Sinewave Indicator gives entry and exit signals 1/16 of a cycle period in advance of the cycle turning point.
- The Sinewave Indicator seldom gives false whipsaw signals when the market is in a Trend Mode.

CHAPTER 12

Adapting to the Trend

"I have no idea," said Tom thoughtlessly.

At this point, I have developed enough tools for you that you can now start putting them together to create some serious trading strategies. This chapter gives you the beginning of one such strategy. You can use this strategy as a beginning and add your own rules to increase the percentage winners.

In previous chapters, I derived and adapted oscillator-type indicators with the goal of having the indicators move with the cycle component of the market with as little lag as possible. Most technical analysis trend-following techniques don't use oscillators; they use moving averages or some variation thereof. In this chapter I will show you how to use the cycle measurement both as a trend indicator and as a trading system.

The slopes from any given point in a cycle to the same point in the next cycle are exactly the same. It doesn't matter whether the point you select is the peak, the valley, or anyplace in between; the slope between the same points in idealized cycles is zero. If there is a difference in the amplitudes between successive samples, either the cycle period has changed or the market is in a trend. Since the cycle periods morph very slowly from cycle to cycle, it is more likely that the one-cycle momentum is an indication of the trend.

Our approach to forming this trading strategy is to measure the Dominant Cycle period and then use that measured period to take a one-cycle momentum. Momentum functions are notoriously noisy, so I smooth the momentum using the three-pole Super Smoother filter described in the next chapter. It is just that simple. The EasyLanguage and eSignal Formula Script (EFS) codes to compute the Smoothed Adaptive Momentum are shown in Figures 12.1 and 12.2, respectively.

```
{**********************************************************
                Smoothed Adaptive Momentum
**********************************************************}
Inputs: Price((H+L)/2),
        alpha(.07),
        Cutoff(8);

Vars:   Smooth(0),
        Cycle(0),
        Q1(0),
        I1(0),
        DeltaPhase(0),
        MedianDelta(0),
        DC(0),
        InstPeriod(0),
        Period(0),
        Num(0),
        Denom(0),
        a1(0),
        b1(0),
        c1(0),
        coef1(0),
        coef2(0),
        coef3(0),
        coef4(0),
        Filt3(0);

Smooth = (Price + 2*Price[1] + 2*Price[2]
    + Price[3])/6;
Cycle = (1 - .5*alpha)*(1 - .5*alpha)*(Smooth
    - 2*Smooth[1] + Smooth[2]) + 2*(1 - alpha)*Cycle[1]
    - (1 - alpha)*(1 - alpha)*Cycle[2];
If currentbar < 7 then Cycle = (Price - 2*Price[1]
    + Price[2]) / 4;

Q1 = (.0962*Cycle + .5769*Cycle[2] - .5769*Cycle[4]
    - .0962*Cycle[6])*(.5 + .08*InstPeriod[1]);
I1 = Cycle[3];

If Q1 <> 0 and Q1[1] <> 0 then DeltaPhase = (I1/Q1
    - I1[1]/Q1[1]) / (1 + I1*I1[1]/(Q1*Q1[1])));
```

FIGURE 12.1 EasyLanguage Code to Compute the Smoothed Adaptive Momentum

```
If DeltaPhase < 0.1 then DeltaPhase = 0.1;
If DeltaPhase > 1.1 then DeltaPhase = 1.1;
MedianDelta = Median(DeltaPhase, 5);

If MedianDelta = 0 then DC = 15 else DC = 6.28318
    / MedianDelta + .5;

InstPeriod = .33*DC + .67*InstPeriod[1];
Period = .15*InstPeriod + .85*Period[1];

Value1 = Price - Price[IntPortion(Period - 1)];

a1 = expvalue(-3.14159 / Cutoff);
b1 = 2*a1*Cosine(1.738*180 / Cutoff);
c1 = a1*a1;
coef2 = b1 + c1;
coef3 = -(c1 + b1*c1);
coef4 = c1*c1;
coef1 = 1 - coef2 - coef3 - coef4;

Filt3 = coef1*Value1 + coef2*Filt3[1] + coef3*Filt3[2]
    + coef4*Filt3[3];
If CurrentBar < 4 then Filt3 = Value1;

Plot1(Filt3, "Filt3");
Plot2(0, "Ref");
```

FIGURE 12.1   *(Continued)*

```
/************************************************************
Title:        Smoothed Adaptive Momentum Indicator
Coded By:  Chris D. Kryza (Divergence Software, Inc.)
Email:   c.kryza@gte.net
Incept:   07/09/2003
Version:   1.0.0

                                          (continued)
```

FIGURE 12.2   EFS Code to Compute the Smoothed Adaptive Momentum

```
=========================================================
Fix History:

07/09/2003 -    Initial Release
1.0.0

=========================================================
*******************************************************/


//External Variables

var nBarCount            = 0;

var aPriceArray          = new Array();
var aSmoothArray         = new Array();
var aCycleArray          = new Array();
var aDeltaPhase          = new Array();
var aPeriod              = new Array();
var aInstPeriod          = new Array();
var aQ1                  = new Array();
var aI1                  = new Array();
var aFiltArray           = new Array();


//== PreMain function required by eSignal to set_
   things up
function preMain() {
var x;

  setPriceStudy(false);
  setStudyTitle("Smoothed Adaptive Momentum");
  setCursorLabelName("Filt3", 0);
  setDefaultBarFgColor( Color.blue, 0 );
  addBand( 0.0, PS_SOLID, 1, Color.black, -10 );

      //initialize arrays
  for (x=0; x<150; x++) {
      aPriceArray[x]      = 0.0;
      aSmoothArray[x]     = 0.0;
      aCycleArray[x]      = 0.0;
      aQ1[x]              = 0.0;
```

FIGURE 12.2   *(Continued)*

```
        aI1[x]                 = 0.0;
        aDeltaPhase[x]         = 0.0;
        aPeriod[x]             = 0.0;
        aInstPeriod[x]         = 0.0;
        aFiltArray[x]          = 0.0;
    }

}

//== Main processing function
function main( Alpha, Cutoff ) {
var x;
var nValue1;
var nDC;
var nOffset;
var nCoef1;
var nCoef2;
var nCoef3;
var nCoef4;
var nA1;
var nB1;
var nC1;
var nMedianDelta;

        //initialize parameters if necessary
        if ( Alpha == null ) {
              Alpha = 0.07;
        }
        if ( Cutoff == null ) {
              Cutoff = 8;
        }


        // study is initializing
   if (getBarState() == BARSTATE_ALLBARS) {
     return null;
   }

        //on each new bar, save array values
        if ( getBarState() == BARSTATE_NEWBAR ) {

              nBarCount++;
```
(continued)

FIGURE 12.2 *(Continued)*

```
            aPriceArray.pop();
            aPriceArray.unshift( 0 );

            aSmoothArray.pop();
            aSmoothArray.unshift( 0 );

            aCycleArray.pop();
            aCycleArray.unshift( 0 );

            aQ1.pop();
            aQ1.unshift( 0 );

            aI1.pop();
            aI1.unshift( 0 );

            aDeltaPhase.pop();
            aDeltaPhase.unshift( 0 );

            aInstPeriod.pop();
            aInstPeriod.unshift( 0 );

            aPeriod.pop();
            aPeriod.unshift( 0 );

            aFiltArray.pop();
            aFiltArray.unshift( 0 );

        }

    aPriceArray[0] = ( high()+low() ) / 2;

    aSmoothArray[0] = ( aPriceArray[0]
        + 2*aPriceArray[1] + 2*aPriceArray[2]
        + aPriceArray[3] ) / 6;

    if ( nBarCount < 7 ) {
            aCycleArray[0] = ( aPriceArray[0]
                - 2*aPriceArray[1] + aPriceArray[2] )
                / 4;
    }
    else {
```

FIGURE 12.2   (Continued)

```
            aCycleArray[0] = ( 1 - 0.5*Alpha )
                * ( 1 - 0.5*Alpha )
                * ( aSmoothArray[0]
                - 2*aSmoothArray[1]
                + aSmoothArray[2] ) + 2*( 1-Alpha )
                * aCycleArray[1] - ( 1-Alpha )
                * ( 1-Alpha ) * aCycleArray[2];
        }

    aQ1[0] = ( 0.0962*aCycleArray[0]
        + 0.5769*aCycleArray[2]
        - 0.5769*aCycleArray[4]
        - 0.0962*aCycleArray[6] ) * ( 0.5 + 0.08
        * aInstPeriod[1] );
    aI1[0] = aCycleArray[3];

    if ( aQ1[0] != 0 && aQ1[1] != 0 ) {
        aDeltaPhase[0] = (aI1[0]/aQ1[0]
            - aI1[1]/aQ1[1]) / (1 + aI1[0]
            *aI1[1]/(aQ1[0]*aQ1[1]));
    }
    if ( aDeltaPhase[0] < 0.1 ) aDeltaPhase[0]
        = 0.1;
    if ( aDeltaPhase[0] > 1.1 ) aDeltaPhase[0]
        = 1.1;

    nMedianDelta = Median( 5, aDeltaPhase );

    if ( nMedianDelta == 0 ) {
        nDC = 15;
    }
    else {
        nDC = 6.28318 / nMedianDelta + 0.5;
    }

    aInstPeriod[0] = 0.33 * nDC + 0.67
        * aInstPeriod[1];
    aPeriod[0] = 0.15*aInstPeriod[0]
        + 0.85*aPeriod[1];


    nOffset = Math.floor( aPeriod[0] )-1;
```
(continued)

FIGURE 12.2   *(Continued)*

```
      if ( nOffset < 0 ) nOffset = 0;

      nValue1 = aPriceArray[0]
         - aPriceArray[ nOffset ];

      nA1 = Math.exp( -3.14159 / Cutoff );
      nB1 = 2*nA1 * Math.cos(  DegToRad( 1.738 * 180
         / Cutoff )  );
      nC1 = nA1 * nA1;

      nCoef2 = nB1 + nC1;
      nCoef3 = -( nC1 + nB1 * nC1 );
      nCoef4 = nC1 * nC1;
      nCoef1 = 1 - nCoef2 - nCoef3 - nCoef4;

      if ( nBarCount < 4 ) {
            aFiltArray[0] = nValue1;
      }
      else {
            aFiltArray[0] = nCoef1*nValue1
               + nCoef2*aFiltArray[1]
               + nCoef3*aFiltArray[2]
               + nCoef4*aFiltArray[3];
      }



      //return the calculated values
      if (!isNaN( aFiltArray[0] ) ) {
            return( aFiltArray[0] );
      }


}


//== Convert Degrees to Radians
function DegToRad( nValue ) {
var nTmp;

      nTmp = nValue * ( Math.PI / 180 );
      return( nTmp );
```

FIGURE 12.2   *(Continued)*

```
}

//== Convert Radians to Degrees
function RadToDeg( nValue ) {
var nTmp;

        nTmp = nValue * ( 180 / Math.PI );

        return( nTmp );

}

function Median( nBars, aArray ) {
var aTmp = new Array();
var nTmp;
var result;
var x;

        //transfer elements to temp array
        x = 0;
        while( x < nBars ) {
                aTmp[x] = aArray[x++];
        }
        //sort array in asc order
        aTmp.sort( SortAsc );


        //if odd # of elements, just take middle
        if ( nBars % 2 != 0 ) {
                result = aTmp[ (nBars+1) / 2 ]
                aTmp = null;
                return( result );
        }
        //if even # elements, take average of two middle
            elements
        else {
                nTmp = nBars/2;
                result = (aTmp[nTmp] + aTmp[nTmp+1])/2;
                aTmp = null;
                return ( result );
        }
}
```
                                          (continued)

FIGURE 12.2   *(Continued)*

```
function SortAsc( arg1, arg2 ) {
      if (arg1<arg2) {
        return( -1 )
      }
      else {
         return( 1 );
      }
}
```

FIGURE 12.2   *(Continued)*

Figure 12.3 suggests that the uptrend starts when the indicator crosses up through the zero line and a downtrend starts when the indicator crosses down through the zero line.

I converted the Smoothed Adaptive Momentum Indicator to an automatic strategy by writing the trading rules to buy each time the filter crosses up through zero and to sell short each time the filter crosses down through zero. I also added a money management stop. This simple but elegant trend-following automatic trading strategy produced the results shown in Table 12.1. The EasyLanguage and EFS codes for the Smoothed Adaptive Momentum strategy are in Figures 12.4 and 12.5, respectively.

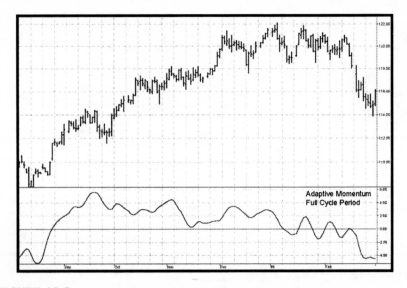

FIGURE 12.3   Smoothed Adaptive Momentum as a Trend Indicator

TABLE 12.1 Sample Trading Results Using the Smoothed Adaptive Momentum Trading Strategy

Future	Net Profit	Number of Trades	Percent Profitable	Profit Factor	Max DD
EC (4/81–3/03)	$112,112	196	40.3%	2.03	($8,137)
JY (9/81–3/03)	$160,950	277	39.7%	2.01	($13,450)
SF (6/76–3/03)	$157,337	523	38.8%	1.64	($13,587)

```
{************************************************************
                Smoothed Adaptive Momentum
*************************************************************}
Inputs: Price((H+L)/2),
        alpha(.07),
        Cutoff(8);

Vars:   Smooth(0),
        Cycle(0),
        Q1(0),
        I1(0),
        DeltaPhase(0),
        MedianDelta(0),
        DC(0),
        InstPeriod(0),
        Period(0),
        Num(0),
        Denom(0),
        a1(0),
        b1(0),
        c1(0),
        coef1(0),
        coef2(0),
        coef3(0),
        coef4(0),
        Filt3(0);

Smooth = (Price + 2*Price[1] + 2*Price[2]
    + Price[3])/6;
Cycle = (1 - .5*alpha)*(1 - .5*alpha)*(Smooth
    - 2*Smooth[1] + Smooth[2]) + 2*(1 - alpha)*Cycle[1]
    - (1 - alpha)*(1 - alpha)*Cycle[2];
                                        (continued)
```

FIGURE 12.4 EasyLanguage Code for the Smoothed Adaptive Momentum Strategy

```
If currentbar < 7 then Cycle = (Price - 2*Price[1]
    + Price[2]) / 4;

Q1 = (.0962*Cycle + .5769*Cycle[2] - .5769*Cycle[4]
    - .0962*Cycle[6])*(.5 + .08*InstPeriod[1]);
I1 = Cycle[3];

If Q1 <> 0 and Q1[1] <> 0 then DeltaPhase = (I1/Q1
    - I1[1]/Q1[1]) / (1 + I1*I1[1]/(Q1*Q1[1])));
If DeltaPhase < 0.1 then DeltaPhase = 0.1;
If DeltaPhase > 1.1 then DeltaPhase = 1.1;
MedianDelta = Median(DeltaPhase, 5);

If MedianDelta = 0 then DC = 15 else DC = 6.28318
    / MedianDelta + .5;

InstPeriod = .33*DC + .67*InstPeriod[1];
Period = .15*InstPeriod + .85*Period[1];

Value1 = Price - Price[IntPortion(Period - 1)];

a1 = expvalue(-3.14159 / Cutoff);
b1 = 2*a1*Cosine(1.738*180 / Cutoff);
c1 = a1*a1;
coef2 = b1 + c1;
coef3 = -(c1 + b1*c1);
coef4 = c1*c1;
coef1 = 1 - coef2 - coef3 -coef4;

Filt3 = coef1*Value1 + coef2*Filt3[1] + coef3*Filt3[2]
    + coef4*Filt3[3];
If CurrentBar < 4 then Filt3 = Value1;

If Filt3 Crosses Over 0 then Buy Next Bar on Open;
If Filt3 Crosses Under 0 then Sell Short Next Bar
    on Open;
```

FIGURE 12.4   *(Continued)*

```
/********************************************************
Title:          Smoothed Adaptive Momentum Trading
                Strategy
Coded By:  Chris D. Kryza (Divergence Software, Inc.)
Email:  c.kryza@gte.net
Incept:  07/09/2003
Version:  1.0.0



============================================================
Fix History:

07/09/2003 -    Initial Release
1.0.0


============================================================
********************************************************/


//External Variables

var nBarCount               = 0;

var aPriceArray             = new Array();
var aSmoothArray            = new Array();
var aCycleArray             = new Array();
var aDeltaPhase             = new Array();
var aPeriod                 = new Array();
var aInstPeriod             = new Array();
var aQ1                     = new Array();
var aI1                     = new Array();
var aFiltArray              = new Array();


var nStatus                 = 0;
var nEntryPrice             = 0;
var nStop                   = 0;
var nPVal                   = 0;
var nSVal                   = 0;

var grID                    = 0;
```

                                              (continued)

FIGURE 12.5   EFS for the Smoothed Adaptive Momentum Strategy

```
//== PreMain function required by eSignal to set_
    things up
function preMain() {
var x;

  setPriceStudy( true );
  setStudyTitle("Smoothed Adaptive Momentum
    Strategy");
  setShowCursorLabel( false );

      //initialize arrays
  for (x=0; x<150; x++) {
      aPriceArray[x]     = 0.0;
      aSmoothArray[x]    = 0.0;
      aCycleArray[x]     = 0.0;
      aQ1[x]             = 0.0;
      aI1[x]             = 0.0;
      aDeltaPhase[x]     = 0.0;
      aPeriod[x]         = 0.0;
      aInstPeriod[x]     = 0.0;
      aFiltArray[x]      = 0.0;
  }

}

//== Main processing function
function main( Alpha, Cutoff, StopAmt, PointValue ) {
var x;
var nValue1;
var nDC;
var nOffset;
var nCoef1;
var nCoef2;
var nCoef3;
var nCoef4;
var nA1;
var nB1;
var nC1;
var nMedianDelta;

      //initialize parameters if necessary
      if ( Alpha == null ) {
```

FIGURE 12.5   *(Continued)*

```
            Alpha = 0.07;
    }
    if ( Cutoff == null ) {
            Cutoff = 8;
    }
    if ( StopAmt == null ) {
            StopAmt = 1000.0;
    }
    if ( PointValue == null ) {
            PointValue = 50;
    }

    nSVal = StopAmt;
    nPVal = PointValue;

    // study is initializing
if (getBarState() == BARSTATE_ALLBARS) {
  return null;
}

    //on each new bar, save array values
    if ( getBarState() == BARSTATE_NEWBAR ) {

            nBarCount++;

            aPriceArray.pop();
            aPriceArray.unshift( 0 );

            aSmoothArray.pop();
            aSmoothArray.unshift( 0 );

            aCycleArray.pop();
            aCycleArray.unshift( 0 );

            aQ1.pop();
            aQ1.unshift( 0 );

            aI1.pop();
            aI1.unshift( 0 );

            aDeltaPhase.pop();
            aDeltaPhase.unshift( 0 );
```
                                        (continued)

FIGURE 12.5 *(Continued)*

```
            aInstPeriod.pop();
            aInstPeriod.unshift( 0 );

            aPeriod.pop();
            aPeriod.unshift( 0 );

            aFiltArray.pop();
            aFiltArray.unshift( 0 );


        }

        aPriceArray[0] = ( high()+low() ) / 2;

        aSmoothArray[0] = ( aPriceArray[0]
            + 2*aPriceArray[1] + 2*aPriceArray[2]
            + aPriceArray[3] ) / 6;

        if ( nBarCount < 7 ) {
            aCycleArray[0] = ( aPriceArray[0]
                - 2*aPriceArray[1] + aPriceArray[2] )
                / 4;
        }
        else {
            aCycleArray[0] = ( 1 - 0.5*Alpha )
                * ( 1 - 0.5*Alpha )
                * ( aSmoothArray[0]
                - 2*aSmoothArray[1]
                + aSmoothArray[2] ) + 2*( 1-Alpha )
                * aCycleArray[1] - ( 1-Alpha )
                * ( 1-Alpha ) * aCycleArray[2];
        }

        aQ1[0] = ( 0.0962*aCycleArray[0]
            + 0.5769*aCycleArray[2]
            - 0.5769*aCycleArray[4]
            - 0.0962*aCycleArray[6] ) * ( 0.5 + 0.08
            * aInstPeriod[1] );
        aI1[0] = aCycleArray[3];

        if ( aQ1[0] != 0 && aQ1[1] != 0 ) {
            aDeltaPhase[0] = (aI1[0]/aQ1[0]
```

FIGURE 12.5   *(Continued)*

```
                       - aI1[1]/aQ1[1]) / (1
                       + aI1[0]*aI1[1]/(aQ1[0]*aQ1[1]));
      }
      if ( aDeltaPhase[0] < 0.1 ) aDeltaPhase[0]
          = 0.1;
      if ( aDeltaPhase[0] > 1.1 ) aDeltaPhase[0]
          = 1.1;

      nMedianDelta = Median( 5, aDeltaPhase );

      if ( nMedianDelta == 0 ) {
           nDC = 15;
      }
      else {
           nDC = 6.28318 / nMedianDelta + 0.5;
      }

      aInstPeriod[0] = 0.33 * nDC + 0.67
          * aInstPeriod[1];
      aPeriod[0] = 0.15*aInstPeriod[0]
          + 0.85*aPeriod[1];

      nOffset = Math.floor( aPeriod[0] )-1;
      if ( nOffset < 0 ) nOffset = 0;

      nValue1 = aPriceArray[0]
          - aPriceArray[ nOffset ];

      nA1 = Math.exp( -3.14159 / Cutoff );
      nB1 = 2*nA1 * Math.cos(  DegToRad( 1.738 * 180
          / Cutoff )  );
      nC1 = nA1 * nA1;

      nCoef2 = nB1 + nC1;
      nCoef3 = -( nC1 + nB1 * nC1 );
      nCoef4 = nC1 * nC1;
      nCoef1 = 1 - nCoef2 - nCoef3 - nCoef4;

      if ( nBarCount < 4 ) {
           aFiltArray[0] = nValue1;
      }
      else {
                                               (continued)
```

FIGURE 12.5 *(Continued)*

```
            aFiltArray[0] = nCoef1*nValue1
               + nCoef2*aFiltArray[1]
               + nCoef3*aFiltArray[2]
               + nCoef4*aFiltArray[3];
   }

   // if currently flat, look for a trade entry
   if ( nStatus == 0 ) {

         if ( nStatus <= 0 && aFiltArray[0]
            > 0 && aFiltArray[1] <= 0 ) {
               goLong();
         }
         else if ( nStatus >= 0 && aFiltArray[0]
            < 0 && aFiltArray[1] >= 0 ) {
               goShort();
         }

   }
   else {

         // in a long trade
         if ( nStatus == 1 ) {

               // if stop hit, sell long
               if ( low() <= nStop ) {
                     if ( open() <= nStop ) {
                           closeLong( open() );
                     }
                     else {
                           closeLong( nStop );
                     }
               }
               // check for reversal signal
               else if ( aFiltArray[0]
                  < 0 && aFiltArray[1] >= 0 ) {
                     goShort();
               }
         }
         // in a short trade
         else if ( nStatus == -1 ) {
```

FIGURE 12.5   *(Continued)*

```
                        // if stop hit, cover short
                        if ( high() >= nStop ) {
                                if ( open() >= nStop ) {
                                        closeShort( open() );
                                }
                                else {
                                        closeShort( nStop );
                                }
                        }
                        // check for reversal signal
                        else if ( aFiltArray[0]
                            > 0 && aFiltArray[1] <= 0 ) {
                                goLong();
                        }
                }

        }


}


//== gID function assigns unique identifier to
    graphic/text routines
function gID() {
  grID ++;
  return( grID );
}

//== Convert Degrees to Radians
function DegToRad( nValue ) {
var nTmp;

        nTmp = nValue * ( Math.PI / 180 );
        return( nTmp );
}

//== Convert Radians to Degrees
function RadToDeg( nValue ) {
var nTmp;


                                              (continued)
```

FIGURE 12.5 *(Continued)*

```
        nTmp = nValue * ( 180 / Math.PI );

        return( nTmp );

}

function Median( nBars, aArray ) {
var aTmp = new Array();
var nTmp;
var result;
var x;

        //transfer elements to temp array
        x = 0;
        while( x < nBars ) {
                aTmp[x] = aArray[x++];
        }
        //sort array in asc order
        aTmp.sort( SortAsc );


        //if odd # of elements, just take middle
        if ( nBars % 2 != 0 ) {
                result = aTmp[ (nBars+1) / 2 ]
                aTmp = null;
                return( result );
        }
        //if even # elements, take average of two middle
           elements
        else {
                nTmp = nBars/2;
                result = (aTmp[nTmp] + aTmp[nTmp+1])/2;
                aTmp = null;
                return ( result );
        }
}


function SortAsc( arg1, arg2 ) {
    if (arg1<arg2) {
      return( -1 )
    }
```

FIGURE 12.5   *(Continued)*

```
      else {
        return( 1 );
      }
}


//enter a short trade
function goShort() {
      drawShapeRelative(1, high(1), Shape.
          DOWNARROW, "",
          Color.maroon, Shape.ONTOP|Shape.BOTTOM,_
              gID());
      Strategy.doShort("Short", Strategy.MARKET,
          Strategy.NEXTBAR, Strategy.DEFAULT );
      nEntryPrice         = open(1);
      nStop               = ( nEntryPrice + nSVal
                              / nPVal );
      nStatus             = -1;
}


//close a short trade
function closeShort( nPrice ) {
      drawShapeRelative(0, low(), Shape.UPARROW, "",
          Color.blue, Shape.ONTOP|Shape.BOTTOM, gID());
      Strategy.doCover("Short Stopped Out",
      Strategy.STOP, Strategy.THISBAR, Strategy.ALL,
          nPrice );
      nStatus             = 0;
}



//enter a long trade
function goLong() {
      drawShapeRelative(1, low(1),  Shape.UPARROW, "",
          Color.lime, Shape.ONTOP|Shape.TOP, gID());
      Strategy.doLong("Long", Strategy.MARKET,_
          Strategy.NEXTBAR, Strategy.DEFAULT );
      nEntryPrice         = open(1);
      nStop               = ( nEntryPrice - nSVal
                              / nPVal );
      nStatus             = 1;
}
```

(continued)

FIGURE 12.5   *(Continued)*

```
//close a long trade
function closeLong( nPrice ) {
      drawShapeRelative(0, high(),  Shape._
         DOWNARROW, "",
      Color.blue, Shape.ONTOP|Shape.TOP, gID());
      Strategy.doSell("Long Stopped Out",_
         Strategy.STOP, Strategy.THISBAR,_
         Strategy.ALL, nPrice);
      nStatus            = 0;
}
```

FIGURE 12.5   *(Continued)*

KEY POINTS TO REMEMBER

- It really does matter if you measure the Dominant Cycle.
- The trend component is measured by taking the momentum across one full Dominant Cycle.

CHAPTER 13

Super Smoothers

"That evens it out," said Tom smoothly.

A method of smoothing called *regularization* was introduced to traders by Dr. Chris Satchwell.[1] He starts with an exponential moving average as

$$F = \alpha * G + (1 - \alpha) * F[1] \qquad (13.1)$$

Where F[1] means the value of F one sample ago. This is EasyLanguage notation. If Equation 13.1 is collected on one side of the equation and squared as in Equation 13.2, and differentiation with respect to F is performed, then its minimum coincides with Equation 13.1. This shows that the exponential moving average can be derived by minimizing an associated function. In equation 13.2, D denotes differentiation.

$$D(F - \alpha * G - (1 - \alpha) * F[1])^2 / D(F) = 0 \qquad (13.2)$$

A least-squares component of an error function can be derived from the argument of the numerator of Equation 13.2 and a penalty term for the curvature can be introduced to achieve regularization. The penalty term comes from the mathematics of finite differences, where the second part of Equation 13.3 is based on the second derivative of F with respect to time.

$$E = (F - \alpha * G - (1 - \alpha) * F[1])^2 + \lambda * (F - 2 * F[1] + F[2])^2 \qquad (13.3)$$

Differentiating Equation 13.3 with respect to F and equating to 0 gives

$$2 * (F - \alpha * G - (1 - \alpha) * F[1]) + 2 * \lambda * (F - 2 * F[1] + F[2]) = 0 \qquad (13.4)$$

Rearranging, Equation 13.4 is written more conveniently as

$$F = (\alpha * G + (1 - \alpha + 2 * \lambda) * F[1] - \lambda * F[2])/(1 + \lambda) \tag{13.5}$$

There are no explicit constraints on the value of the regularization constant λ. However, just a small amount of experimentation shows that unreasonable results can be obtained if the regularization constant is too large. For example, Figure 13.1 shows the transfer response of the Regularized filter for $\alpha = 0.33$ and $\lambda = 10$. In this case, the filter has more than a 6-dB gain at a frequency of 0.03 cycles per day (a 33-bar cycle). That means that the 33-bar period components in the input waveform will be amplified rather than smoothed.

It is ideal if the frequency components we want to pass through the filter are not amplified at all and the frequency components we want to reject are attenuated by the filter. The ideal goal is approximately met in a Regularized filter if the relationship between alpha and lambda is maintained as

$$\lambda = \text{expvalue}\,(0.16/\alpha) \tag{13.6}$$

For example, if $\alpha = 0.33$, then the ideal value of lambda is 1.624. The filter transfer response for this pair of parameters is shown in Figure 13.2.

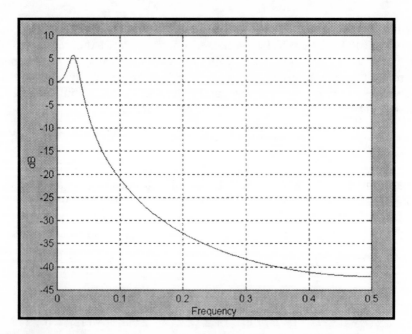

FIGURE 13.1   Transfer Response of the Regularized Filter ($\alpha = 0.33$, $\lambda = 10$)

The frequency response is almost flat from zero frequency to 0.05 cycles per day. From that point on, the higher-frequency components are increasingly attenuated.

One amazing characteristic of Regularized filters is that their zero-frequency lag is determined solely by the alpha parameter, regardless of the value of lambda that is used. An example of the Regularized filter lag response is shown in Figure 13.3 for the ideal value of lambda. The relationship of the zero-frequency lag and alpha in an exponential moving average is

$$\alpha = \frac{1}{\text{Lag} + 1} \tag{13.7}$$

It therefore follows that if the zero-frequency lag is 2, then $\alpha = 0.33$ and vice versa.

Recalling from Chapter 2 that the transfer response of an exponential moving average is expressed as

$$H(z) = \frac{\text{Output}}{\text{Input}} = \frac{\alpha}{1 - (1 - \alpha) * Z^{-1}} \tag{13.8}$$

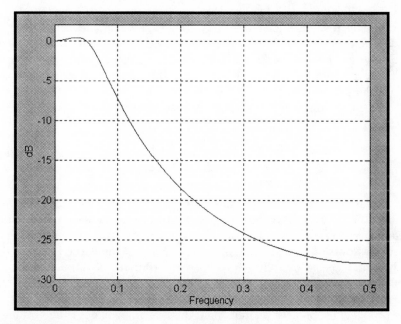

FIGURE 13.2 Transfer Response of the Regularized Filter ($\alpha = 0.33$, $\lambda = 1.624$)

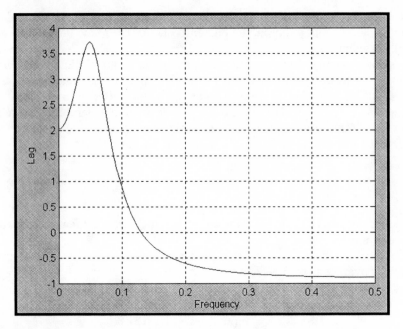

FIGURE 13.3 Lag Response of the Regularized Filter ($\alpha = 0.33$, $\lambda = 1.624$)

If the delay factor Z^{-1} is $1/(1 - \alpha)$, the denominator goes to 0 and thus the transfer response goes to infinity. This is called a *pole of the transfer response*. Don't worry: Since α must be less than unity, and since the delay can only have integer values, the pole condition is never attained—rather it is a descriptor of the transfer response. In this case, the denominator is a first-order polynomial of Z^{-1}.

The Regularized filter transfer response is written as

$$H(z) = \frac{\text{Output}}{\text{Input}} = \frac{\dfrac{\alpha}{1 + \lambda}}{1 - \dfrac{(1 - \alpha + 2\lambda)}{1 + \lambda} Z^{-1} + \dfrac{\lambda}{1 + \lambda} Z^{-2}} \qquad (13.9)$$

Equation 13.9 shows that the transfer response now has a second-order polynomial in the denominator. From the fundamental theorem of algebra, we know that an Nth-order polynomial can be factored into N roots. Roots of a polynomial are those values of the variable where the polynomial goes to 0. Therefore, an Nth-ordered polynomial produces N poles in the transfer response of a filter. The more poles a filter has, the sharper its attenuation curve becomes with respect to frequency. Visualize the transfer response as a circus tent; the filtering you get is like rolling a marble off the tent without actually getting to a tent pole. The more poles you have in the tent, the faster you can make the marble roll. The fact that the Regularized filter has one more pole than an exponential moving average is why it has superior smoothing.

The flat transfer response of an idealized Regularized filter and its being derived by taking multiple derivatives are reminiscent of Butterworth filters. Butterworth filters are analog filters (as opposed to digital filters) that are called *maximally flat* because the first N derivatives of an Nth-ordered Butterworth filter are 0 at zero frequency.

BUTTERWORTH DIGITAL FILTERS

Years ago I translated analog Butterworth filters to their digital approximations. The transfer response is characterized by a single variable—the cutoff frequency. The cutoff frequency is that frequency where the input is attenuated by 3 dB. Below the cutoff frequency, the input frequency components are passed to the output; above the cutoff frequency, the input frequency components are rejected to the extent possible by the filter characteristics. Since traders are more comfortable with period, which is the reciprocal of frequency, the equations for the Butterworth digital filters are characterized in terms of the cutoff period.

The equations for a two-pole Butterworth digital filter, in Easy-Language notation, are

$$
\begin{aligned}
&a = \text{ExpValue } (-1.414 * 3.14159/\text{Cutoff}); \\
&b = 2 * a * \text{Cosine } (1.414 * 180/\text{Cutoff}); \\
&\text{Butter} = ((1 - b + a * a)/4) * (\text{Price} + 2 * \text{Price}[1] + \text{Price}[3]) \\
&\qquad\qquad + b * \text{Butter}[1] + a * a * \text{Butter}[2];
\end{aligned} \qquad (13.10)
$$

The EasyLanguage and eSignal Formula Script (EFS) codes to implement the two-pole Butterworth digital filter are given in Figures 13.4 and 13.5, respectively.

It may be more convenient for some readers to implement the filter as a function of a given Cutoff Period. Table 13.1 is provided for this case. In a prior work,[2] I have also given tables for Gaussian filters.

As opposed to the Regularized filter, the order of Butterworth filters can be increased indefinitely to increase the sharpness of the filter rejection. For traders, this quickly reaches the point of diminishing returns because increasing the number of poles in the filter means the lag of the filter is also increased. A three-pole filter gives just about the limit of tolerable lag for a selected cutoff period. The equations for a three-pole Butterworth filter, in EasyLanguage format, are

```
{*******************************************************
                Two Pole Butterworth Filter
********************************************************}

Inputs: Price((H+L)/2),
        Period(15);

Vars:   a1(0),
        b1(0),
        coef1(0),
        coef2(0),
        coef3(0),
        Butter(0);

a1 = expvalue(-1.414*3.14159 / Period);
b1 = 2*a1*Cosine(1.414*180 / Period);
coef2 = b1;
coef3 = -a1*a1;
coef1 = (1 - b1 + a1*a1) / 4;

Butter = coef1*(Price + 2*Price[1] + Price[3])
    + coef2*Butter[1] + coef3*Butter[2];
If CurrentBar < 3 then Butter = Price;

Plot1(Butter, "Butter");
```

FIGURE 13.4 EasyLanguage Code to Compute the Two-Pole Butterworth Filter

$$a = \text{ExpValue } (-3.14159/\text{Cutoff});$$
$$b = 2 * a * \text{Cosine } (1.738 * 180/\text{Cutoff});$$
$$c = a * a;$$
$$\begin{aligned}\text{Butter} = {}& ((1 - b + c) * (1 - c)/8) * (\text{Price} + 3 * \text{Price}[1] \quad (13.11)\\
& + 3 * \text{Price}[3] + \text{Price}[4])\\
& + (b + c) * \text{Butter}[1] - (c + b * c)\\
& * \text{Butter}[2] + c * c * \text{Butter}[3];\end{aligned}$$

The EasyLanguage and EFS codes to implement the three-pole Butterworth digital filter are given in Figures 13.6 and 13.7, respectively.

Table 13.2 lists the coefficients of three-pole Butterworth filters as a function of their cutoff period. It is provided as a convenience for readers who may want only to quickly access the coefficient values rather than compute them.

```
/***********************************************************
Title:  2 Pole Butterworth Filter
Coded By:  Chris D. Kryza (Divergence Software, Inc.)
Email:  c.kryza@gte.net
Incept:  07/09/2003
Version:  1.0.0



===========================================================
Fix History:

07/09/2003 -    Initial Release
1.0.0


===========================================================
***********************************************************/


//External Variables
var nPrice          = 0;
var nBarCount       = 0;

var aPriceArray     = new Array();
var aButterArray    = new Array();


//== PreMain function required by eSignal to set
   things up
function preMain() {
var x;

  setPriceStudy(true);
  setStudyTitle("2-Pole Butterworth");
  setCursorLabelName("Butter", 0);
  setDefaultBarFgColor( Color.blue, 0 );

      //initialize arrays
  for (x=0; x<10; x++) {
      aPriceArray[x]          = 0.0;
      aButterArray[x]         = 0.0;
  }
```

(continued)

FIGURE 13.5   EFS Code for the Two-Pole Butterworth Filter

```
}

//== Main processing function
function main( Period ) {
var x;
var nA1;
var nB1;
var nCoef1;
var nCoef2;
var nCoef3;

      //initialize parameters if necessary
      if ( Period == null ) {
            Period = 15;
      }

      // study is initializing
   if (getBarState() == BARSTATE_ALLBARS) {
     return null;
   }

      //on each new bar, save array values
      if ( getBarState() == BARSTATE_NEWBAR ) {

            nBarCount++;

            aPriceArray.pop();
            aPriceArray.unshift( 0 );

            aButterArray.pop();
            aButterArray.unshift( 0 );

      }

      nPrice = ( high()+low() ) / 2;
      aPriceArray[0] = nPrice;


      nA1 = Math.exp( -1.414 * 3.14159 / Period );
      nB1 = 2*nA1 * Math.cos( DegToRad( 1.414 * 180
          / Period ) );
```

FIGURE 13.5   *(Continued)*

```
      nCoef2 = nB1;
      nCoef3 = -nA1 * nA1;
      nCoef1 = ( 1 - nB1 + nA1 * nA1 ) / 4;

      if ( nBarCount < 3 ) {
            aButterArray[0] = aPriceArray[0];
      }
      else {
            aButterArray[0] = nCoef1*( aPriceArray[0]
                + 2*aPriceArray[1] + aPriceArray[2] )
                + nCoef2*aButterArray[1]
                + nCoef3*aButterArray[2];
      }


      //return the calculated values
      if ( !isNaN( aButterArray[0] ) ) {
            return( aButterArray[0] );
      }


}



//== Convert Degrees to Radians
function DegToRad( nValue ) {
var nTmp;

      nTmp = nValue * ( Math.PI / 180 );
      return( nTmp );
}
```

FIGURE 13.5   *(Continued)*

TABLE 13.1 Two-Pole Butterworth Filter Coefficients

Y = A[0] * X[0] + A[1] * X[1] + A[2] * X[2] + B[1] * Y[1] + B[2] * Y[2];

Cutoff Period	A[0]	A[1]	A[2]	B[1]	B[2]
2	0.285784	0.571568	0.285784	−0.131366	−0.011770
4	0.203973	0.407946	0.203973	0.292597	−0.108489
6	0.130825	0.261650	0.130825	0.704171	−0.227470
8	0.088501	0.177002	0.088501	0.975372	−0.329377
10	0.063284	0.126567	0.063284	1.158161	−0.411296
12	0.047322	0.094643	0.047322	1.287652	−0.476938
14	0.036654	0.073308	0.036654	1.383531	−0.530147
16	0.029198	0.058397	0.029198	1.457120	−0.573914
18	0.023793	0.047586	0.023793	1.515266	−0.610438
20	0.019754	0.039507	0.019754	1.562309	−0.641324
22	0.016658	0.033317	0.016658	1.601119	−0.667753
24	0.014235	0.028470	0.014235	1.633667	−0.690607
26	0.012303	0.024607	0.012303	1.661342	−0.710555
28	0.010739	0.021477	0.010739	1.685157	−0.728112
30	0.009454	0.018908	0.009454	1.705862	−0.743678
32	0.008386	0.016773	0.008386	1.724025	−0.757571
34	0.007490	0.014980	0.007490	1.740086	−0.770045
36	0.006729	0.013459	0.006729	1.754388	−0.781305
38	0.006079	0.012158	0.006079	1.767204	−0.791520
40	0.005518	0.011037	0.005518	1.778753	−0.800827

```
{*********************************************************
            Three Pole Butterworth Filter
 *********************************************************}

Inputs: Price((H+L)/2),
        Period(15);

Vars:   a1(0),
        b1(0),
        c1(0),
        coef1(0),
        coef2(0),
        coef3(0),
        coef4(0),
        Butter(0);

a1 = expvalue(-3.14159 / Period);
b1 = 2*a1*Cosine(1.738*180 / Period);
c1 = a1*a1;
```

FIGURE 13.6 EasyLanguage Code to Compute the Three-Pole Butterworth Filter

```
coef2 = b1 + c1;
coef3 = -(c1 + b1*c1);
coef4 = c1*c1;
coef1 = (1 - b1 +c1)*(1 - c1) / 8;

Butter = coef1*(Price + 3*Price[1] + 3*Price[2]
    + Price[3]) + coef2*Butter[1] + coef3*Butter[2]
    + coef4*Butter[3];
If CurrentBar < 4 then Butter = Price;

Plot1(Butter, "Butter");
```

FIGURE 13.6 *(Continued)*

```
/********************************************************
Title:  3 Pole Butterworth Filter
Coded By:  Chris D. Kryza (Divergence Software, Inc.)
Email:  c.kryza@gte.net
Incept:  07/09/2003
Version:  1.0.0



=========================================================
Fix History:

07/09/2003 -   Initial Release
1.0.0


=========================================================
********************************************************/


//External Variables
var nPrice          = 0;
var nBarCount       = 0;

var aPriceArray     = new Array();
var aButterArray    = new Array();
```

(continued)

FIGURE 13.7 EFS Code to Compute the Three-Pole Butterworth Filter

```
//== PreMain function required by eSignal to set
    things up
function preMain() {
var x;

  setPriceStudy(true);
  setStudyTitle("3-Pole Butterworth");
  setCursorLabelName("Butter", 0);
  setDefaultBarFgColor( Color.blue, 0 );

      //initialize arrays
  for (x=0; x<10; x++) {
      aPriceArray[x]                = 0.0;
      aButterArray[x]               = 0.0;
  }

}

//== Main processing function
function main( Period ) {
var x;
var nCoef1;
var nCoef2;
var nCoef3;
var nCoef4;
var nA1;
var nB1;
var nC1;


      //initialize parameters if necessary
      if ( Period == null ) {
             Period = 15;
      }

      // study is initializing
  if (getBarState() == BARSTATE_ALLBARS) {
    return null;
  }

      //on each new bar, save array values
      if ( getBarState() == BARSTATE_NEWBAR ) {
```

FIGURE 13.7   *(Continued)*

```
        nBarCount++;

        aPriceArray.pop();
        aPriceArray.unshift( 0 );

        aButterArray.pop();
        aButterArray.unshift( 0 );

}

nPrice = ( high()+low() ) / 2;
aPriceArray[0] = nPrice;


nA1 = Math.exp( -3.14159 / Period );
nB1 = 2*nA1 * Math.cos( DegToRad( 1.738 * 180
    / Period ) );
nC1 = nA1 * nA1;

nCoef2 = nB1 + nC1;
nCoef3 = -( nC1 + nB1 * nC1 );
nCoef4 = nC1 * nC1;
nCoef1 = ( 1 - nB1 + nC1 ) * ( 1 - nC1 ) / 8;

if ( nBarCount < 4 ) {
        aButterArray[0] = aPriceArray[0];
}
else {
        aButterArray[0] = nCoef1
            * ( aPriceArray[0]
            + 3*aPriceArray[1] + 3*aPriceArray[2]
            + aPriceArray[3] )
            + nCoef2*aButterArray[1]
            + nCoef3*aButterArray[2]
            + nCoef4*aButterArray[3];
}



//return the calculated values
if ( !isNaN( aButterArray[0] ) ) {
        return( aButterArray[0] );
```
(continued)

FIGURE 13.7   *(Continued)*

```
            }


    }


    //== Convert Degrees to Radians
    function DegToRad( nValue ) {
    var nTmp;

            nTmp = nValue * ( Math.PI / 180 );
            return( nTmp );
    }
```

FIGURE 13.7   *(Continued)*

TABLE 13.2   Three-Pole Butterworth Filter Coefficients

Y = A[0] * X[0] + A[1] * X[1] + A[2] * X[2] + A[3] * X[3] + B[1] * Y[1] + B[2] * Y[2]
+ B[3] * Y[3];

Cutoff Period	A[0]	A[1]	A[2]	A[3]	B[1]	B[2]	B[3]
2	0.170149	0.510448	0.510448	0.170149	−0.336246	−0.026816	0.001867
4	0.100733	0.302200	0.302200	0.100733	0.398405	−0.247486	0.043214
6	0.050373	0.151118	0.151118	0.050373	1.080990	−0.607116	0.123145
8	0.027610	0.082830	0.082830	0.027610	1.505892	−0.934652	0.207880
10	0.016541	0.049622	0.049622	0.016541	1.783327	−1.200263	0.284610
12	0.010629	0.031887	0.031887	0.010629	1.976163	−1.412114	0.350920
14	0.007213	0.021640	0.021640	0.007213	2.117205	−1.582459	0.407548
16	0.005111	0.015334	0.015334	0.005111	2.224560	−1.721388	0.455938
18	0.003750	0.011250	0.011250	0.003750	2.308883	−1.836396	0.497514
20	0.002831	0.008492	0.008492	0.002831	2.376806	−1.932941	0.533488
22	0.002188	0.006565	0.006565	0.002188	2.432658	−2.015013	0.564848
24	0.001726	0.005179	0.005179	0.001726	2.479376	−2.085571	0.592385
26	0.001385	0.004156	0.004156	0.001385	2.519020	−2.146834	0.616731
28	0.001128	0.003385	0.003385	0.001128	2.553078	−2.200500	0.638395
30	0.000931	0.002794	0.002794	0.000931	2.582648	−2.247883	0.657784
32	0.000778	0.002333	0.002333	0.000778	2.608560	−2.290012	0.675232
34	0.000656	0.001967	0.001967	0.000656	2.631451	−2.327708	0.691011
36	0.000558	0.001674	0.001674	0.000558	2.651819	−2.361631	0.705347
38	0.000479	0.001437	0.001437	0.000479	2.670059	−2.392315	0.718425
40	0.000414	0.001242	0.001242	0.000414	2.686486	−2.420202	0.730403

MULTIPOLE SMOOTHING FILTERS

The transfer responses of Butterworth filters have polynomials in both the numerator and denominator. For example, the transfer response of a two-pole Butterworth filter is

$$H(z) = \frac{\text{Output}}{\text{Input}} = \frac{A[0] + A[1]Z^{-1} + A[2]Z^{-2}}{1 + B[1]Z^{-1} + B[2]Z^{-2}} \tag{13.12}$$

There is a polynomial in the numerator as well as the denominator. The significance of the polynomial in the numerator is that it represents the finite impulse response (FIR) part of the filter. This part is like a simple moving average. The denominator forms the iterative part of the filter calculation and is the infinite impulse response (IIR) part of the filter. The FIR part of the filter sharpens the filter rejection response, but it also contributes to lag in the response. Recognizing that the parts of a Butterworth filter are separable, I form the multipole super smoothing filters by simply deleting the polynomial in the numerator. Since the transfer response must be unity when $Z^{-1} = -1$, I replace the polynomial with the fixed coefficient $C[0] = 1 - B[1] + B[2]$. The EasyLanguage and EFS codes for the two-pole Super Smoother are given in Figures 13.8 and 13.9, respectively. The coefficients are in Table 13.3.

The transfer response of the two-pole Super Smoother is shown in Figure 13.10. Note that it is almost identical to the transfer response of the Regularized filter shown in Figure 13.2. The difference between the two is that the characteristics of the Super Smoother are determined by a single parameter and the flatness of the passband response is guaranteed.

The order of Super Smoother filters can be increased indefinitely to increase the sharpness of the filter rejection, just as with Butterworth filters. The EasyLanguage and EFS codes to implement the three-pole Super Smoother filter are given in Figures 13.11 and 13.12, respectively.

Table 13.4 lists the coefficients of three-pole Super Smoother filters as a function of their cutoff period. It is provided as a convenience for readers who may want only to quickly access the coefficient values rather than compute them.

Figure 13.13 shows that a three-pole Super Smoother filter has far more attenuation in the reject band than the two-pole filters of Figures 13.2 and 13.10. The passbands are identical in all three cases.

```
{*********************************************************
                  Two Pole Super Smoother
*******************************************************}

Inputs: Price((H+L)/2),
        Period(15);

Vars:   a1(0),
        b1(0),
        coef1(0),
        coef2(0),
        coef3(0),
        Filt2(0);

a1 = expvalue(-1.414*3.14159 / Period);
b1 = 2*a1*Cosine(1.414*180 / Period);
coef2 = b1;
coef3 = -a1*a1;
coef1 = 1 - coef2 - coef3;

Filt2 = coef1*Price + coef2*Filt2[1] + coef3*Filt2[2];
If CurrentBar < 3 then Filt2 = Price;

Plot1(Filt2, "Filt2");
```

FIGURE 13.8 EasyLanguage Code to Compute the Two-Pole Super Smoother Filter

```
/*********************************************************
Title:  Two Pole Super Smoother
Coded By:  Chris D. Kryza (Divergence Software, Inc.)
Email:  c.kryza@gte.net
Incept:  07/09/2003
Version:  1.0.0



=========================================================
Fix History:

07/09/2003 -   Initial Release
1.0.0
```

FIGURE 13.9 EFS Code to Compute the Two-Pole Super Smoother Filter

```
=========================================================
**********************************************************/


//External Variables
var nPrice                 = 0;
var nBarCount              = 0;

var aPriceArray            = new Array();
var aFiltArray             = new Array();


//== PreMain function required by eSignal to set_
    things up
function preMain() {
var x;

  setPriceStudy(true);
  setStudyTitle("2-Pole Super Smoother");
  setCursorLabelName("Filt2", 0);
  setDefaultBarFgColor( Color.blue, 0 );

      //initialize arrays
  for (x=0; x<10; x++) {
      aPriceArray[x]       = 0.0;
      aFiltArray[x]        = 0.0;
  }

}

//== Main processing function
function main( Period ) {
var x;
var nA1;
var nB1;
var nCoef1;
var nCoef2;
var nCoef3;


      //initialize parameters if necessary
      if ( Period == null ) {
            Period = 15;
```

(continued)

FIGURE 13.9   (Continued)

```
        }

        // study is initializing
    if (getBarState() == BARSTATE_ALLBARS) {
      return null;
    }

        //on each new bar, save array values
        if ( getBarState() == BARSTATE_NEWBAR ) {

                nBarCount++;

                aPriceArray.pop();
                aPriceArray.unshift( 0 );

                aFiltArray.pop();
                aFiltArray.unshift( 0 );

        }

        nPrice = ( high()+low() ) / 2;
        aPriceArray[0] = nPrice;


        nA1 = Math.exp( -1.414 * 3.14159 / Period );
        nB1 = 2*nA1 * Math.cos( DegToRad( 1.414 * 180_
            / Period ) );

        nCoef2 = nB1;
        nCoef3 = -nA1 * nA1;
        nCoef1 = 1 - nCoef2 - nCoef3;

        if ( nBarCount < 3 ) {
                aFiltArray[0] = aPriceArray[0];
        }
        else {
                aFiltArray[0] = nCoef1*aPriceArray[0]_
                    + nCoef2*aFiltArray[1]
                    + nCoef3*aFiltArray[2];
        }
        //return the calculated values
        if ( !isNaN( aFiltArray[0] ) ) {
                return( aFiltArray[0] );
```

FIGURE 13.9   *(Continued)*

```
        }


}


//== Convert Degrees to Radians
function DegToRad( nValue ) {
var nTmp;

        nTmp = nValue * ( Math.PI / 180 );
        return( nTmp );
}
```

FIGURE 13.9   *(Continued)*

TABLE 13.3   Two-Pole Super Smoother Coefficients

Y = C[0] * X[0] + B[1] * Y[1] + B[2] * Y[2];			
Cutoff Period	**C[0]**	**B[1]**	**B[2]**
2	1.143136	−0.13137	−0.01177
4	0.815892	0.292597	−0.10849
6	0.523299	0.704171	−0.22747
8	0.354005	0.975372	−0.32938
10	0.253135	1.158161	−0.4113
12	0.189286	1.287652	−0.47694
14	0.146616	1.383531	−0.53015
16	0.116794	1.45712	−0.57391
18	0.095172	1.515266	−0.61044
20	0.079015	1.562309	−0.64132
22	0.066634	1.601119	−0.66775
24	0.05694	1.633667	−0.69061
26	0.049213	1.661342	−0.71056
28	0.042955	1.685157	−0.72811
30	0.037816	1.705862	−0.74368
32	0.033546	1.724025	−0.75757
34	0.029959	1.740086	−0.77005
36	0.026917	1.754388	−0.78131
38	0.024316	1.767204	−0.79152
40	0.022074	1.778753	−0.80083

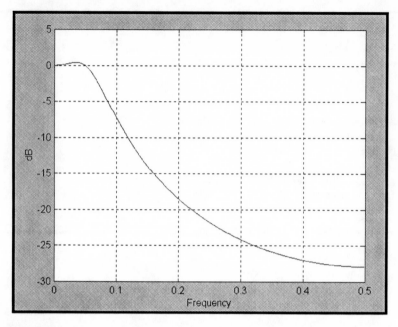

FIGURE 13.10 Transfer Response of the Two-Pole Super Smoother Filter

```
{*********************************************************
               Three Pole Super Smoother
 *******************************************************}

Inputs: Price((H+L)/2),
        Period(15);

Vars:   a1(0),
        b1(0),
        c1(0),
        coef1(0),
        coef2(0),
        coef3(0),
        coef4(0),
        Filt3(0);

a1 = expvalue(-3.14159 / Period);
```

FIGURE 13.11 EasyLanguage Code to Compute the Three-Pole Super Smoother Filter

```
b1 = 2*a1*Cosine(1.738*180 / Period);
c1 = a1*a1;
coef2 = b1 + c1;
coef3 = -(c1 + b1*c1);
coef4 = c1*c1;
coef1 = 1 - coef2 - coef3 - coef4;

Filt3 = coef1*Price + coef2*Filt3[1] + coef3*Filt3[2]
    + coef4*Filt3[3];
If CurrentBar < 4 then Filt3 = Price;

Plot1(Filt3, "Filt3");
```

FIGURE 13.11 *(Continued)*

```
/********************************************************
Title:  Three Pole Super Smoother
Coded By:  Chris D. Kryza (Divergence Software, Inc.)
Email:  c.kryza@gte.net
Incept:  07/09/2003
Version: 1.0.0


===========================================================
Fix History:

07/09/2003 -    Initial Release
1.0.0


===========================================================
********************************************************/


//External Variables
var nPrice                  = 0;
var nBarCount               = 0;

var aPriceArray             = new Array();
var aFiltArray              = new Array();
                                             (continued)
```

FIGURE 13.12 EFS Code to Compute the Three-Pole Super Smoother Filter

```
//== PreMain function required by eSignal to set_
    things up
function preMain() {
var x;

  setPriceStudy(true);
  setStudyTitle("3-Pole Super Smoother");
  setCursorLabelName("Filt3", 0);
  setDefaultBarFgColor( Color.blue, 0 );

      //initialize arrays
  for (x=0; x<10; x++) {
      aPriceArray[x]              = 0.0;
      aFiltArray[x]               = 0.0;
  }

}

//== Main processing function
function main( Period ) {
var x;
var nA1;
var nB1;
var nC1;
var nCoef1;
var nCoef2;
var nCoef3;
var nCoef4;


      //initialize parameters if necessary
      if ( Period == null ) {
            Period = 15;
      }

      // study is initializing
  if (getBarState() == BARSTATE_ALLBARS) {
    return null;
  }

      //on each new bar, save array values
      if ( getBarState() == BARSTATE_NEWBAR ) {
```

FIGURE 13.12   *(Continued)*

```
        nBarCount++;

        aPriceArray.pop();
        aPriceArray.unshift( 0 );

        aFiltArray.pop();
        aFiltArray.unshift( 0 );

    }

    nPrice = ( high()+low() ) / 2;
    aPriceArray[0] = nPrice;


    nA1 = Math.exp( -3.14159 / Period );
    nB1 = 2*nA1 * Math.cos( DegToRad( 1.738 * 180
        / Period ) );
    nC1 = nA1 * nA1;

    nCoef2 = nB1 + nC1;
    nCoef3 = -( nC1 + nB1 * nC1 );
    nCoef4 = nC1 * nC1;
    nCoef1 = 1 - nCoef2 - nCoef3 - nCoef4;

    if ( nBarCount < 3 ) {
        aFiltArray[0] = aPriceArray[0];
    }
    else {
        aFiltArray[0] = nCoef1*aPriceArray[0]
            + nCoef2*aFiltArray[1]
            + nCoef3*aFiltArray[2]
            + nCoef4*aFiltArray[3];
    }



    //return the calculated values
    if ( !isNaN( aFiltArray[0] ) ) {
        return( aFiltArray[0] );
    }

}
```

(continued)

FIGURE 13.12 *(Continued)*

```
//== Convert Degrees to Radians
function DegToRad( nValue ) {
var nTmp;

        nTmp = nValue * ( Math.PI / 180 );
        return( nTmp );
}
```

FIGURE 13.12   (Continued)

TABLE 13.4   Three-Pole Super Smoother Filter Coefficients

Y = C[0] * X[0] + B[1] * Y[1] + B[2] * Y[2] + B[3] * Y[3];

Cutoff Period	C[0]	B[1]	B[2]	B[3]
2	1.361195	−0.33625	−0.02682	0.001867
4	0.805867	0.398405	−0.24749	0.043214
6	0.402981	1.08099	−0.60712	0.123145
8	0.22088	1.505892	−0.93465	0.20788
10	0.132326	1.783327	−1.20026	0.28461
12	0.085031	1.976163	−1.41211	0.35092
14	0.057706	2.117205	−1.58246	0.407548
16	0.04089	2.22456	−1.72139	0.455938
18	0.029999	2.308883	−1.8364	0.497514
20	0.022647	2.376806	−1.93294	0.533488
22	0.017507	2.432658	−2.01501	0.564848
24	0.01381	2.479376	−2.08557	0.592385
26	0.011083	2.51902	−2.14683	0.616731
28	0.009027	2.553078	−2.2005	0.638395
30	0.007451	2.582648	−2.24788	0.657784
32	0.00622	2.60856	−2.29001	0.675232
34	0.005246	2.631451	−2.32771	0.691011
36	0.004465	2.651819	−2.36163	0.705347
38	0.003831	2.670059	−2.39232	0.718425
40	0.003313	2.686486	−2.4202	0.730403

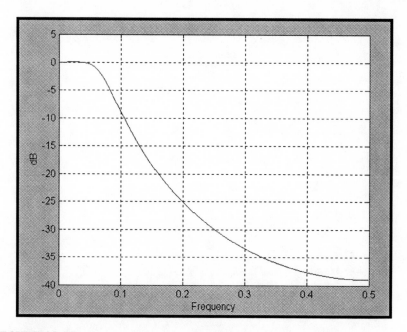

FIGURE 13.13   Transfer Response of a Three-Pole Super Smoother Filter

KEY POINTS TO REMEMBER

- A Regularized filter has smoothing superior to that of an exponential moving average because an extra pole in the transfer response is introduced.
- The α and λ parameters of the Regularized filters can be independently assigned.
- The optimum relationship between α and λ for a flat passband response is approximately $\alpha = \exp(0.16/\lambda)$.
- A Butterworth filter is an analog filter whose response is maximally flat at zero frequency.
- A Butterworth digital filter is generated via an approximate translation from the analog version.
- Butterworth filters can have an arbitrarily large number of poles.
- The passband of Butterworth filters is prescribed by a single parameter. That parameter is the Cutoff Period, where the attenuation of the filter is 3 dB.
- The Super Smoother filter is formed by retaining the IIR part of a Butterworth digital filter.
- You can return to this chapter for equations to compute smoothing filters or to look up tables of their coefficients.

CHAPTER 14

Time Warp—
Without Space
Travel

"I only get Newsweek,*" said Tom timelessly.*

O ne of the most frustrating aspects of technical analysis is trying to avoid whipsaw trades. When the moving averages are made smoother to avoid these whipsaws, the lag produced by the smoothing often renders the signals ineffective. The dilemma therefore is how to strike a balance between the amount of smoothing that can be obtained and the amount of lag that can be tolerated. In this chapter, I introduce a new tool to address the smoothing versus lag problem more effectively. In particular, you will learn another way to create better smoothing filters.

A moving average is a simple concept involving sampled data. One averages the data over the last N samples, moves forward one sample and averages over the new set of N samples, and so on. For each new set of N samples, only the oldest sample is discarded and one new sample is added. The average is done over a fixed number of samples and moved forward one sample at a time. In this way the average moves. An engineer views the process differently. From this perspective, the data moves down a fixed delay line that is tapped to get the output of each sample, and the tap outputs are added together to produce the moving average. This process is depicted in the schematic of Figure 14.1 for a four-bar moving average. In Figure 14.1, the symbol Z^{-1} means that there is one unit of delay. In the case of daily data, the delay would be one day. The filter response in terms of the Z transform is

$$H(z) = 1 + Z^{-1} + Z^{-2} + Z^{-3} \qquad (14.1)$$

213

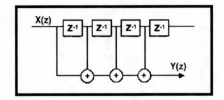

FIGURE 14.1   Schematic of a Moving Average

The equation for the moving average, in EasyLanguage format, is

$$\text{Filt} = (\text{Price} + \text{Price}[1] + \text{Price}[2] + \text{Price}[3])/4; \qquad (14.2)$$

That is, successively older data samples from the newest sample are averaged to obtain the filtered output. The tapped delay line concept is favored by engineers because more generalized finite impulse response (FIR) filters can be developed by changing the relative amplitudes of the samples. For example, if we wanted the middle two samples to have twice the weight of the newest sample and oldest sample in our four-sample example, the schematic diagram would be as shown in Figure 14.2.

The equation for the FIR filter, in EasyLanguage format, is

$$\text{Filt} = (\text{Price} + 2 * \text{Price}[1] + 2 * \text{Price}[2] + \text{Price}[3])/6; \qquad (14.3)$$

This is exactly the same filter used to eliminate the two-bar and three-bar cycle components in Figure 4.1. The multipliers on price are called the *coefficients* of the filter. Note that the filter is always normalized to the sum of the coefficients. This normalization is done so that the output will be the same as the input if all the samples have the same value. In engineering terms, the direct current, or zero frequency (DC) gain is equal to unity. The FIR filter can be made to have additional smoothing by making the filter longer. However, the lag of a FIR filter is approximately half the filter length. The result is that if we want greater smoothing we must accept the additional lag in conventional filters.

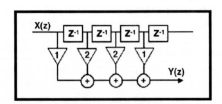

FIGURE 14.2   Schematic of a Four-Element FIR Filter

Conventional filters use the Z transform to describe the filter transfer characteristic, where Z^{-1} denotes a unit delay. There are a semi-infinite number of orthonormal functions for transform arithmetic. One such function is formed from Laguerre polynomials. The mathematical expression for a kth-order Laguerre transfer response is

$$H(z) = \frac{1-\gamma}{1-\gamma Z^{-1}} \left[\frac{Z^{-1}-\gamma}{1-\gamma Z^{-1}} \right]^{k-1} \tag{14.4}$$

The Laguerre transform can be represented as an exponential moving average (EMA) low-pass filter (the first term) followed by a succession of all-pass elements instead of unit delays (the $k-1$ terms). All terms have exactly the same damping factor γ. We see that these are all pass networks by examining the frequency response. When frequency is 0, the Z^{-1} term has a value of 1, and therefore the element evaluates to $(1.-\gamma)/(1.-\gamma) = 1$. Similarly, when frequency is infinite, Z^{-1} has a value of -1, and therefore the element evaluates to $(-1.-\gamma)/(1.+\gamma) = -1$. The element has a unity gain at all frequencies between 0 and infinity, and therefore is an all-pass network. However, the phase from input to output shifts over the frequency range, causing the lag to be variable as a function of frequency. The degree to which the lag is variable depends on the value of the damping factor γ. For example, the lag, or group delay, for $\gamma = 0.6$ and $\gamma = 0.8$ is shown in Figure 14.3.

Therefore, we can make a filter using the Laguerre elements instead of the unit delay, whose coefficients are also [1 2 2 1]/6 as with the FIR filter. The difference is that we have warped the time between the delay line taps. The schematic of the Laguerre filter is shown in Figure 14.4.

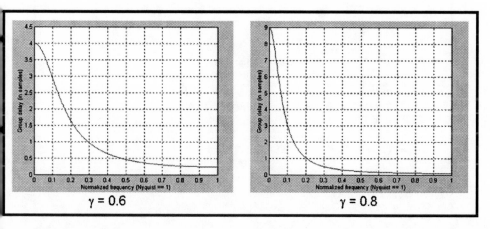

$\gamma = 0.6$ \qquad $\gamma = 0.8$

FIGURE 14.3 All-Pass Network Lag Is a Function of Frequency and Damping Factor

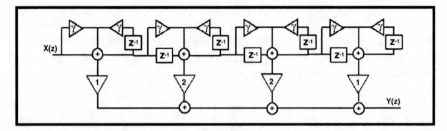

FIGURE 14.4   Schematic of a Laguerre Filter

The EasyLanguage and eSignal Formula Script (EFS) codes for a four-element Laguerre Filter are given in Figures 14.5 and 14.6, respectively. L0 is the output of the first section and is just an EMA. The following three sections are identical in their form. The four sections of the Laguerre delay line are summed exactly the same way as a linear delay line for a FIR filter. The Laguerre output is the Filt variable. An identical-length FIR filter is also computed for comparison.

```
Inputs:     Price((H+L)/2),
            gamma(.8);

Vars:       L0(0),
            L1(0),
            L2(0),
            L3(0),
            Filt(0)
            FIR(0);

L0 = (1 - gamma)*Price + gamma*L0[1];
L1 = -gamma*L0 + L0[1] + gamma*L1[1];
L2 = -gamma*L1 + L1[1] + gamma*L2[1];
L3 = -gamma*L2 + L2[1] + gamma*L3[1];

Filt = (L0 + 2*L1 + 2*L2 + L3) / 6;
FIR = (Price + 2*Price[1] + 2*Price[2] + Price[3]) / 6;

Plot1(Filt, "Filt");
Plot2(FIR, "FIR");
```

FIGURE 14.5   EasyLanguage Code for the Laguerre Filter

```
/*******************************************************
Title:        Laguerre Filter
Coded By:   Chris D. Kryza (Divergence Software, Inc.)
Email:     c.kryza@gte.net
Incept:   06/19/2003
Version:   1.0.0


=========================================================
Fix History:

06/19/2003 -    Initial Release
1.0.0


=========================================================
*******************************************************/


//External Variables
var aL0                      = new Array();
var aL1                      = new Array();
var aL2                      = new Array();
var aL3                      = new Array();
var aPriceArray              = new Array();

//== PreMain function required by eSignal to set_
   things up
function preMain() {
var x;

    setPriceStudy(true);
    setStudyTitle("LaguerreFilter");
    setCursorLabelName("Filt", 0);
    setCursorLabelName("FIR", 1);
    setDefaultBarFgColor( Color.blue, 0 );
    setDefaultBarFgColor( Color.red,  1 );

        //initialize arrays
    for (x=0; x<5; x++) {
            aPriceArray[x]     = 0.0;
            aL0[x]             = 0.0;
            aL1[x]             = 0.0;
                                    (continued)
```

FIGURE 14.6 EFS Code for the Laguerre Filter

```
                aL2[x]              = 0.0;
                aL3[x]              = 0.0;
        }


}

//== Main processing function
function main( Gamma ) {
var x;
var nFilt;
var nFIR;

        //initialize parameters if necessary
        if ( Gamma == null ) {
                Gamma = 0.80;
        }

        // study is initializing
    if (getBarState() == BARSTATE_ALLBARS) {
      return null;
    }

        //on each new bar, save array values
        if ( getBarState() == BARSTATE_NEWBAR ) {

                aPriceArray.pop();
                aPriceArray.unshift( 0 );

                aL0.pop();
                aL0.unshift( 0 );

                aL1.pop();
                aL1.unshift( 0 );

                aL2.pop();
                aL2.unshift( 0 );

                aL3.pop();
                aL3.unshift( 0 );

        }
```

FIGURE 14.6   *(Continued)*

```
aPriceArray[0] = ( high()+low() ) / 2;
aL0[0] = (1.0-Gamma) * aPriceArray[0]
    + Gamma*aL0[1];
aL1[0] = -Gamma*aL0[0] + aL0[1] + Gamma*aL1[1];
aL2[0] = -Gamma*aL1[0] + aL1[1] + Gamma*aL2[1];
aL3[0] = -Gamma*aL2[0] + aL2[1] + Gamma*aL3[1];

//calculate LaGuerre filter
nFilt = ( aL0[0] + 2*aL1[0] + 2*aL2[0]
    + aL3[0] ) / 6;
//calculate FIR filter
nFIR = ( aPriceArray[0] + 2*aPriceArray[1]
    + 2*aPriceArray[2] + aPriceArray[3] ) / 6;


//return the calculated values
if ( !isNaN( nFilt ) ) {
        return new Array( nFilt, nFIR );
}


}
```

FIGURE 14.6   *(Continued)*

The results of the Laguerre and FIR filters are shown in Figure 14.7. Remember that all filters have identical lengths. The FIR filter has a lag of only 1.5 bars and only moderately smooths the price data. On the other hand, the Laguerre filter is dramatically smoother and also has significant lag. You can decrease the smoothing and the lag by decreasing the damping factor. When the damping factor is reduced to 0, the Laguerre filter is identical to the FIR filter. This is a simple way to control the action of a moving average and still use only a few data samples in the calculation.

The story does not end with conventional filters. As I am fond of saying, "Truth and science always triumph over ignorance and superstition." If we can generate superior smoothing with very short filters, it follows that we should be able to create superior indicators using very short data lengths also. The use of shorter data lengths means that we can make the indicators more responsive to changes in the price. The Laguerre RSI will be used as an example.

Welles Wilder defined the RSI as

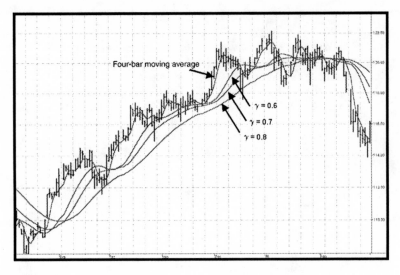

FIGURE 14.7 Four-Element Laguerre Filter Is Dramatically Smoother than a Conventional Four-Element FIR Filter

$$RSI = 100 - 100/(1 + RS)$$

$$\text{where } RS = (\text{Closes Up})/(\text{Closes Down})$$
$$= CU/CD$$

RS is shorthand for Relative Strength. That is, CU is the sum of the difference in closing prices over the observation period where that difference is positive. Similarly, CD is the sum of the difference in closing prices over the observation period where that difference is negative, but the sum is expressed as a positive number. When we substitute CU/CD for RS and simplify the RSI equation, we get

$$RSI = 100 - \frac{100}{1 + \dfrac{CU}{CD}}$$

$$= 100 - \frac{100CD}{CU + CD}$$

$$= \frac{100CU + 100CD - 100CD}{CU + CD}$$

$$RSI = \frac{100CU}{CU + CD}$$

In other words, the RSI is the percentage of the sum of the delta closes up to the sum of all the delta closes over the observation period. In the EasyLanguage and EFS codes of Figures 14.8 and 14.9, respectively, I have generated an RSI over Laguerre time rather than linear time, using only four data samples. In this case, I used a damping factor of 0.5, but you can adjust the damping factor to best suit your own data.

An example of the results for the four-element Laguerre RSI is shown in Figure 14.10 below the price charts. The 20 percent and 80 percent signal levels are also plotted. Note that the excursions of the RSI are typically lock to lock and that the recovery is rapid at each major price reversal. A typical use of the Laguerre RSI is to buy after the line crosses back over the

```
Inputs:     gamma(.5);

Vars:       L0(0),
            L1(0),
            L2(0),
            L3(0),
            CU(0),
            CD(0),
            RSI(0);

L0 = (1 - gamma)*Close + gamma*L0[1];
L1 = - gamma *L0 + L0[1] + gamma *L1[1];
L2 = - gamma *L1 + L1[1] + gamma *L2[1];
L3 = - gamma *L2 + L2[1] + gamma *L3[1];

CU = 0;
CD = 0;
If L0 >= L1 then CU = L0 - L1 Else CD = L1 - L0;
If L1 >= L2 then CU = CU + L1 - L2 Else CD = CD + L2
    - L1;
If L2 >= L3 then CU = CU + L2 - L3 Else CD = CD + L3
    - L2;

If CU + CD <> 0 then RSI = CU / (CU + CD);

Plot1(RSI, "RSI");
Plot2(.8);
Plot3(.2);
```

FIGURE 14.8   EasyLanguage Code to Compute a Laguerre RSI Indicator

```
/***********************************************************
Title:        Laguerre RSI Indicator
Coded By:    Chris D. Kryza (Divergence Software, Inc.)
Email:   c.kryza@gte.net
Incept:   06/19/2003
Version:  1.0.0



===========================================================
Fix History:

06/19/2003 -    Initial Release
1.0.0


===========================================================
***********************************************************/


//External Variables
var aL0                          = new Array();
var aL1                          = new Array();
var aL2                          = new Array();
var aL3                          = new Array();
var aPriceArray                  = new Array();
var nRSI                         = 0;

//== PreMain function required by eSignal to set_
   things up
function preMain() {
var x;

    setPriceStudy(false);
    setStudyTitle("LaguerreRSI");
    setCursorLabelName("RSI", 0);
    setDefaultBarFgColor( Color.blue, 0 );
    addBand( 0.80, PS_SOLID, 2, Color.black, -55 );
    addBand( 0.20, PS_SOLID, 2, Color.black, -56 );

       //initialize arrays
    for (x=0; x<5; x++) {
            aPriceArray[x]  = 0.0;
```

FIGURE 14.9   EFS Code to Compute a Laguerre RSI Indicator

```
                aL0[x]                    = 0.0;
                aL1[x]                    = 0.0;
                aL2[x]                    = 0.0;
                aL3[x]                    = 0.0;
        }

}

//== Main processing function
function main( Gamma ) {
var x;
var nCD;
var nCU;

        //initialize parameters if necessary
        if ( Gamma == null ) {
                Gamma = 0.50;
        }

        // study is initializing
   if (getBarState() == BARSTATE_ALLBARS) {
        return null;
   }

        //on each new bar, save array values
        if ( getBarState() == BARSTATE_NEWBAR ) {

                aPriceArray.pop();
                aPriceArray.unshift( 0 );

                aL0.pop();
                aL0.unshift( 0 );

                aL1.pop();
                aL1.unshift( 0 );

                aL2.pop();
                aL2.unshift( 0 );

                aL3.pop();
                aL3.unshift( 0 );
                                                (continued)
```

FIGURE 14.9   *(Continued)*

```
    }
    aPriceArray[0] = close();
    aL0[0] = (1.0-Gamma) * aPriceArray[0] + Gamma
        *aL0[1];
    aL1[0] = -Gamma*aL0[0] + aL0[1] + Gamma*aL1[1];
    aL2[0] = -Gamma*aL1[0] + aL1[1] + Gamma*aL2[1];
    aL3[0] = -Gamma*aL2[0] + aL2[1] + Gamma*aL3[1];


    nCU = 0;
    nCD = 0;

    if ( aL0[0] >= aL1[0] ) {
        nCU = aL0[0] -aL1[0];
    }
    else {
        nCD = aL1[0] - aL0[0];
    }

    if ( aL1[0] >= aL2[0] ) {
        nCU = nCU + aL1[0] - aL2[0];
    }
    else {
        nCD = nCD + aL2[0] -  aL1[0];
    }
    if ( aL2[0] >= aL3[0] ) {
        nCU = nCU + aL2[0] - aL3[0];
    }
    else {
        nCD = nCD + aL3[0] - aL2[0];
    }


    if ( nCU + nCD != 0 ) {
        nRSI = nCU / ( nCU + nCD );
    }

    return( nRSI );

}
```

FIGURE 14.9   *(Continued)*

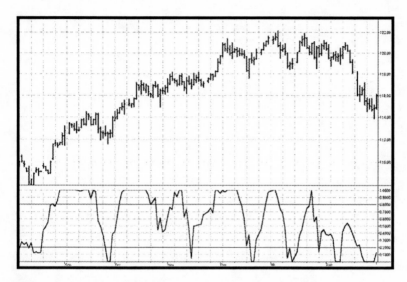

FIGURE 14.10   A Laguerre RSI Reacts Rapidly to Price Changes

20 percent level and sell after the price crosses back down over the 80 percent level. Of course, just as with the conventional RSI, more elaborate trading rules can be created.

KEY POINTS TO REMEMBER

- The Laguerre transform provides a time warp such that the low-frequency components are delayed much more than the high-frequency components.
- Time distortion enables very smooth filters to be built using a short amount of data.
- Indicators can also be created using the time warp.
- Time-warped indicators react faster because a shorter amount of data is used.

CHAPTER 15

Evaluating
Trading Systems

"I got the first three wrong," said Tom forthrightly.

There are basically two ways to trade using technical analysis—discretionarily and systematically. Discretionary traders can, and have, made spectacular amounts of money with their techniques. They integrate their life's experience, knowledge of the markets, and technical indicators to make their trading decisions. In fact, I have used a large fraction of this book to describe new indicators to be used as tools. Systematic traders, on the other hand, do not need to know very much about the market or have much experience. Instead, they rely on the trading signals automatically produced by rules implemented by computer programs. They have the confidence to rely on the computerized systems because the performance statistics can be reproduced by backtesting. That is not to say that hypothetical performance is perfect. There can be sharp differences between hypothetical performance and real trading results. For example, hypothetical trading does not involve financial risk, and the ability to withstand losses or to adhere to a particular trading system in the face of these losses is not considered. Implementation issues, such as slippage and commission, can only be included as allowance factors. Furthermore, the trading system can have performance in the future significantly different from its past performance due simply to the randomness of events. Since backtests are always done with the benefit of hindsight, there are all kinds of ways to cheat on reported performance. This chapter is about what you can realistically expect from your trading system rather than how to cheat the statistics.

Many people equate speculation in the market to gambling. Their beliefs are reinforced by popular books such as *A Random Walk Down*

Wall Street.[1] This belief persists although it is patently false and intellectually dishonest. More serious investors look at fundamental considerations such as P/E ratios, Sales, Debt, and so on, and give scant attention to technical analysis. The technique described in this chapter uses some gaming concepts not only to show that there is merit to trading using technical analysis trading systems, but also to enable you to visualize what equity growth performance you can reasonably expect from your system.

There are a number of statistics that are important if you are putting your hard-earned money at risk. Maximum drawdown is important because it, plus required margin, is the absolute minimum amount of money you should have in your account to avoid a margin call with reasonable probability. The number of consecutive losers is a test of how strong your stomach must be to trade the system. The average profit per trade is important to know because you must cover your transaction costs (commission plus slippage) before you can start making money for yourself.

Taking away all the details of the particular system, there are two statistics that enable you to assess what performance you can expect. These are the percentage of profitable trades and the Profit Factor. It is desirable to have as high a percentage of winners as possible, but this need not be greater than 50 percent to be profitable if you make more on winning trades than you lose on losing trades. Profit Factor is the ratio of Gross Winnings to Gross Losses. In terms of gaming, it is the payout probability. By determining whether a trade is a winner or a loser using the percentage wins and a random number generator, applying the payout probability to each trade, and summing the randomly selected trades, you can provide realistic expectations for the equity growth produced by the system. Only in this sense can randomization be introduced to establish performance. Simply winning or losing is not a random occurrence.

We can create an equity growth simulator and plot the results in an Excel spreadsheet. First we need to insert the two important statistics. In cell A1, type "% Winners" and in cell A2 type 45. In cell B1, type "Profit Factor" and in cell B2 type 1.5. The values of 45 and 1.5 are only initial values. The entries into cells A2 and B2 are system statistics that you can change to visualize their impact on equity growth.

In cell A3 input =RAND(). This creates a random number having a uniform probability density in the range between 0 and 1. This random number is compared to the probability of a win by inserting =IF(A3 < B1/100,B2,0) into cell B3. This conditional statement says that if the random number falls within the winning probability then assign the payout probability (the Profit Factor) to the trade, otherwise assign a value of −1 to the trade. This is the outcome of the trade. In cell C3 input =B3. Copy all of row 3 into row 4. Then change cell C4 to be =C3 + B4. This sums the trades in column C. Next copy all of row 4 and paste into rows 5 through 500. Column C now becomes the equity growth for the randomized set of trades using only the percent winners and Profit Factor. This equity growth changes every time you press F9, causing the spreadsheet to recalculate.

You can plot the equity curve for ease of interpretation. To do this, highlight cells C3 through C500. Then click on the chart wizard and input the data as requested. First, select a line type chart and click on the type shown in the upper left corner of the thumbnail examples. Click Next. Then click Finish. Your chart is done! Now you are free to experiment with the kind of equity growth you can expect from your trading system. Just press F9 to recompute the spreadsheet. You will create a new randomized equity growth curve because all the random numbers have changed. Repeat as often as you desire to get a feeling that you know what to expect. Figures 15.1 and 15.2 are just two examples I ran using the default statistics. Note that although exactly the same statistics are used, the equity curves are dramatically different. The message is that you should not blindly accept an equity curve (real or hypothetical) from a vendor without also finding out what the Profit Factor and Percent Profitable statistics were.

To see what a nice equity growth curve looks like, change cell A2 to 50 and cell B2 to 2.0. MESA Software is among the few systems developers that have systems with statistics such as these. You can see the backtested

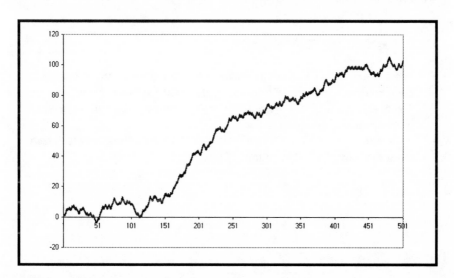

FIGURE 15.1 Hypothetical Equity Growth for %Profitable = 45 and Profit Factor = 1.50

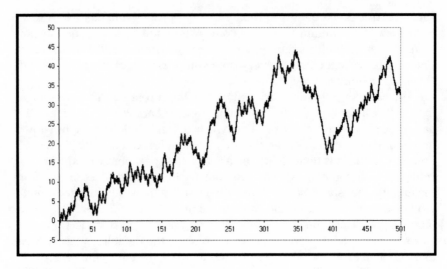

FIGURE 15.2   Another Hypothetical Equity Growth Example for %Profitable = 45 and Profit Factor = 1.50

equity curves of some of our systems at www.mesa-systems.com. Next, explore what the lower-limit statistics might be for a profitable trading system. My experience is that the boundary is 42 in cell A2 (for percentage winners) and 1.5 (for Profit Factor) in cell B2.

KEY POINTS TO REMEMBER

- Profit Factor and Percentage Winners of a trading system are all you need to create a Monte Carlo equity curve of that system.
- A real equity curve is only one of the possibilities that can be produced by a Monte Carlo equity curve.
- A Monte Carlo simulation can be used to evaluate the expected performance of any trading system.

CHAPTER 16

Leading Indicators

"Leading indicators are neat," said Tom predictably.

here are two basic kinds of leading indicators: causal and noncausal filters. Causal filters depend on data and noncausal filters can be predictive from almost any other basis, including gut feelings. The Sinewave Indicator described in Chapter 11 is an example of a noncausal filter. The purpose of this chapter is to derive the limitations and usefulness of causal predictive filters. It is a fundamental principle that causal filters cannot predict a specific event because their very value depends on that event. That is to say, causal filters cannot anticipate a transient response. However, they can and do act as reliable indicators of steady-state responses.

All moving averages have lag. A moving average is depicted as the dashed line relative to the original function (the solid line) in Figure 16.1a. The difference between the two lines d is a constant value in the case of a continuous trend. Similarly, the lag k is also a constant value. The leading indicator is created by adding the difference between the original function and its moving average to the function itself. Adding the difference necessarily places the indicator with a negative lag relative to the original function, as depicted in Figure 16.1b. Negative lag makes this filter a leading indicator. The amount of lead is exactly equal to the amount of lag of the moving average.

Since the amount of lead of the leading indicator is dependent on the lag of a moving average, it is instructive to examine the lag of an exponential moving average as a function of its smoothing parameter alpha. Imagine an original function that increases by 1 with each sample. The function will have a value of I on the Ith sample. If the moving average has a lag of k, then the moving average will have a value of $(I - k)$ on the Ith day.

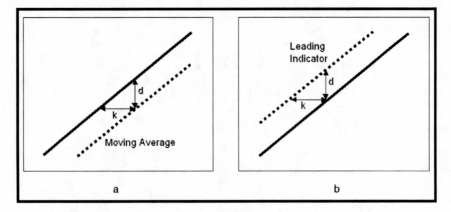

FIGURE 16.1 How Leading Indicators Are Constructed
a. A moving average has a lag *k* and a difference *d*.
b. Adding the moving average difference yields a lead *k*.

Similarly, the moving average will have had a value of $(I - 1 - k)$ on the $(I - 1)$th day. Putting these values in the equation for an exponential moving average, we have

$$(I - k) = \alpha * I + (1 - \alpha) * (I - 1 - k) \qquad (16.1)$$

Solving for alpha in terms of the delay *k*, we have the relationship

$$\alpha = 1/(k + 1) \qquad (16.2)$$

Or, conversely

$$k = 1/\alpha - 1 \qquad (16.3)$$

Equation 16.3 tells how much lead we can expect from our leading indicator. From Chapter 2, the transfer response is the ratio of the output to the input. Thus the transfer response of the leading indicator can be written as

$$H(z) = \frac{\text{Output}}{\text{Input}} = 2 - \frac{\alpha * Z^{-1}}{1 - (1 - \alpha) * Z^{-1}}$$

$$= \frac{2 + (\alpha - 2) * Z^{-1}}{1 - (1 - \alpha) * Z^{-1}} \qquad (16.4)$$

But there is a price to be paid for getting the leading function. That price is noise gain. If we let $Z^{-1} = 1$ in Equation 16.4, we get the zero frequency (constant input) gain. Doing this algebra, the gain of this filter is unity. That is, if the input is constant we get exactly the same output from the filter. The output cannot be leading because there is no trend to the input. Letting $Z^{-1} = -1$, the value of the transfer response at the Nyquist (highest possible) frequency is obtained. Doing this, the filter gain for a two-bar cycle is $(4 - \alpha)/(2 - \alpha)$. So the noise gain varies from 2 when $\alpha = 0$ to 3 when $\alpha = 1$. If the lead is three bars, Equation 16.2 gives $\alpha = 0.25$, and therefore the noise gain is 2.14, slightly more than 6 dB. Figure 16.2 shows how the noise gain varies with frequency for the case when $\alpha = 0.25$.

Noise gain is not a good thing. The noise gain can be reduced by following the leading indicator filter with an exponential moving average. As I indicated earlier, all moving averages have lag. So, if an alpha of the moving average is selected to have less lag than the lead of the leading indicator, an indicator having a net leading function can still be produced. As an example, selecting $\alpha = 0.33$ results in an exponential moving average that has a lag of only two bars. The attenuation at $Z^{-1} = 1$ is 0.2, which gives a greater attenuation than the noise gain of the leading indicator. The net gain of the composite filter is shown in Figure 16.3. While there is still some noise gain in the vicinity of a 20-bar cycle (frequency = 0.05), the net filter has a net smoothing effect over most of the frequency range.

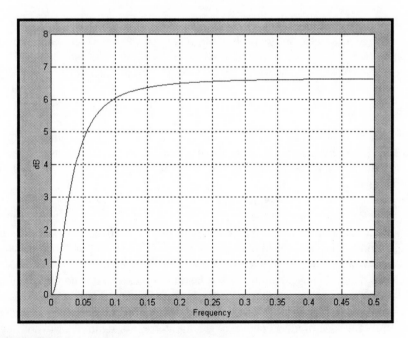

FIGURE 16.2 Noise Gain of a Leading Indicator

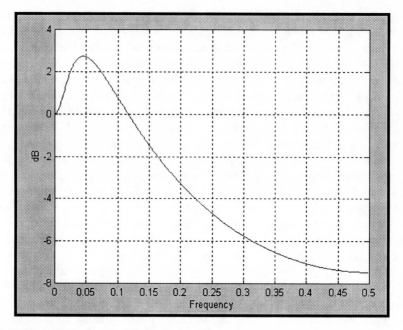

FIGURE 16.3   Net Gain of a Leading Indicator

The leading characteristic is still present in the net filter, as shown in Figure 16.4. As predicted, the lead is one bar at very low frequencies. That is, the trend indication will lead by one bar. However, the net filter has a lag of approximately 2.5 bars for cycle components near 20-bar cycles. Also, higher-frequency lag settles down to be about half a bar. The interpretation of the lag response is that the filter predicts a continuation of a trend by 1 bar, lags abrupt changes by about 0.5 bars, and lags smooth changes that can be fitted by segments of a 20-bar sinewave by as much as 2.5 bars. That's the law of physics—you cannot get something for nothing. Causal filters can have a predictive capability over some portion of the frequency response, but not at all frequencies. There is no magic predictor.

The EasyLanguage and eSignal Formula Script (EFS) codes to compute several leading indicators are given in Figures 16.5 and 16.6, respectively. In these codes, the leading indicator is compared to an exponential moving average whose $\alpha = 0.5$. This exponential moving average has a lag of only a half bar. The relative positions of the leading indicator and the exponential moving average show when the market is in an uptrend or a downtrend as in the example in Figure 16.7. The alphas of the leading indicator are provided as inputs for ease of modification of the indicator. For example, the continuation of the trend is more clearly identified if $\alpha 1$ is reduced to a value of 0.15. The impact of giving the indicator greater lead is shown in Figure 16.8.

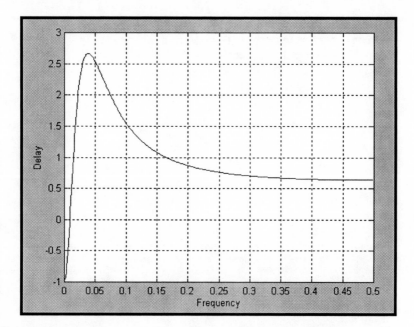

FIGURE 16.4 The Net Filter Has a Low-Frequency Leading Characteristic

```
Inputs: Price((H+L)/2),
        alpha1(.25),
        alpha2(.33);

Vars:   Lead(0),
        NetLead(0),
        EMA(0);

Lead = 2*Price +(alpha1 - 2)*Price[1]
   + (1 - alpha1)*Lead[1];
NetLead = alpha2*Lead + (1 - alpha2)*NetLead[1];

EMA = .5*Price + .5*EMA[1];

Plot1(NetLead, "Lead");
Plot2(EMA, "EMA");
```

FIGURE 16.5 EasyLanguage Code to Compute Leading Indicators

```
*********************************************************
Title:  Leading Indicator
Coded By:  Chris D. Kryza (Divergence Software, Inc.)
Email:  c.kryza@gte.net
Incept:  09/02/2003
Version:  1.0.0



=========================================================
Fix History:

09/02/2003 -    Initial Release
1.0.0


=========================================================
*********************************************************/


//External Variables
var nPrice                 = 0;
var nBarCount              = 0;

var aPriceArray            = new Array();
var aLead                  = new Array();
var aNetLead               = new Array();
var aEMA                   = new Array();


//== PreMain function required by eSignal to set_
   things up
function preMain() {
var x;

  setPriceStudy(true);
  setStudyTitle("Leading Indicator");
  setCursorLabelName("Lead", 0);
  setCursorLabelName("EMA",  1 );
  setDefaultBarFgColor( Color.red,  0 );
  setDefaultBarFgColor( Color.blue, 1 );

      //initialize arrays
  for (x=0; x<10; x++) {
```

FIGURE 16.6   EFS Code to Compute Leading Indicators

```
        aPriceArray[x]              = 0.0;
        aLead[x]                    = 0.0;
        aNetLead[x]                 = 0.0;
        aEMA[x]                     = 0.0;
   }

}

//== Main processing function
function main( Alpha1, Alpha2 ) {
var x;

        //initialize parameters if necessary
        if ( Alpha1 == null ) {
             Alpha1 = 0.25;
        }
        if ( Alpha2 == null ) {
             Alpha2 = 0.33;
        }

        // study is initializing
   if (getBarState() == BARSTATE_ALLBARS) {
     return null;
   }

        //on each new bar, save array values
        if ( getBarState() == BARSTATE_NEWBAR ) {

                nBarCount++;

                aPriceArray.pop();
                aPriceArray.unshift( 0 );

                aLead.pop();
                aLead.unshift( 0 );

                aNetLead.pop();
                aNetLead.unshift( 0 );

                aEMA.pop();
                aEMA.unshift( 0 );

                                        (continued)
```

FIGURE 16.6   (Continued)

```
        }

        nPrice = ( high()+low() ) / 2;
        aPriceArray[0] = nPrice;


        aLead[0] = 2 * aPriceArray[0] + ( Alpha1 - 2.0 )
            * aPriceArray[1] + ( 1.0 - Alpha1 )
            * aLead[1];
        aNetLead[0] = Alpha2 * aLead[0]
            + ( 1.0 - Alpha2 ) * aNetLead[1];

        aEMA[0] = 0.5 * aPriceArray[0] + 0.5 * aEMA[1];


        //return the calculated values
        if ( !isNaN( aNetLead[0] ) && !isNaN( aEMA[0] )
            && nBarCount > 20 ) {
                return new Array( aNetLead[0], aEMA[0] );
        }


}
```

FIGURE 16.6   *(Continued)*

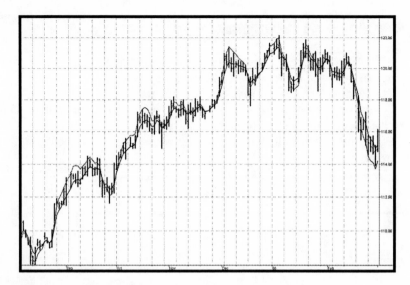

FIGURE 16.7 Leading Indicator ($\alpha 1 = 0.25$, $\alpha 2 = 0.33$) and EMA

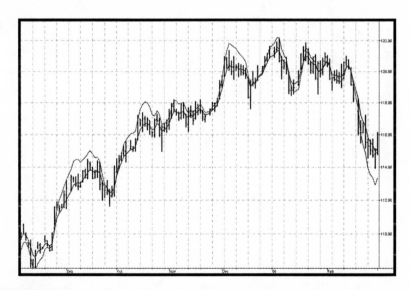

FIGURE 16.8 Leading Indicator ($\alpha 1 = 0.15$, $\alpha 2 = 0.33$) and EMA Provides a Clearer Picture of the Trend Continuation

KEY POINTS TO REMEMBER

- Adding the difference between price and an exponential moving average to the price itself creates a leading indicator.
- The leading indicator always has noise gain.
- Smoothing the leading indicator with another exponential moving average can mitigate noise gain.
- Constants can be selected to provide a net lead for the indicator at low frequencies.
- The leading indicator has a lagging signal at price turning points.

CHAPTER 17

Simplifying Simple Moving Average Computations

"One topic has to be last," said Tom finally.

A simple moving average (SMA) of length N is computed by adding N values and dividing the sum by N. The process is repeated on a bar-by-bar basis. What could be easier? While conceptually easy, the coding for long moving averages can be tedious because there are so many terms. The tedium can be reduced by putting the summation in a loop. But looping is difficult to do in some applications, such as Excel. Another simplifying approach is to drop off the oldest value and add a new value to the moving average. But this requires computing the initial value of the long moving average at least once. I will show you two ways to compute the SMA with ease.

In Z transform notation, a unit delay is represented by Z^{-1}. The transfer response is the output of the filter divided by its input. Thus, the transfer response of an eight-bar SMA would be written as

$$H(z) = (1 + Z^{-1} + Z^{-2} + Z^{-3} + Z^{-4} + Z^{-5} + Z^{-6} + Z^{-7})/8 \qquad (17.1)$$

This same expression, written in EasyLanguage where a delay of N bars is represented in square brackets as [N], is shown in Equation 17.2.

$$\text{SMA} = (\text{Price} + \text{Price}[1] + \text{Price}[2] + \text{Price}[3] + \text{Price}[3]$$
$$+ \text{Price}[4] + \text{Price}[5] + \text{Price}[6] + \text{Price}[7])/8; \qquad (17.2)$$

Equation 17.1 is a simple finite series that can be written most generally in fractional form as

$$H(z) = \frac{Y(z)}{X(z)} = \left(\frac{1 - z^{-N}}{1 - z^{-1}}\right)\Big/(N + 1) \tag{17.3}$$

where $Y(z)$ is the filter output and $X(z)$ is the filter input.

Equation 17.3 is identical to Equation 17.1 if $N = 7$, and is therefore an SMA. When we carry out the cross multiplication of Equation 17.3, we obtain

$$Y(z) = (X(z)(1 - z^{-N}) + Y(z)z^{-1})/(N + 1) \tag{17.4}$$

Equation 17.4 provides the means to program an arbitrarily long SMA using just a few terms. The EasyLanguage equivalent of Equation 17.4 is

$$\text{SMA} = (\text{Price} - \text{Price}[N] + \text{SMA}[1])/(N + 1); \tag{17.5}$$

Another SMA programming trick can be accomplished by recognizing that we don't have to do the filtering all at one time. Rather, we can cascade filters. That means we can filter the output of a previous filter that takes the output of a previous filter, and so on. Cascading filters are represented by multiplication in Z transforms. Therefore, the SMA transfer response of cascaded filters can be written as

$$H(z) = (1 + z^{-1})(1 + z^{-2})(1 + z^{-4}) \ldots (1 + z^{-2^{K-1}})/2^K \tag{17.6}$$

For example, if $K = 3$, we would have an eight-bar SMA. As a test, we can expand Equation 17.6 to be

$$\begin{aligned}
H(z) &= (1 + z^{-1})(1 + z^{-2})(1 + z^{-4})/8 \\
&= (1 + z^{-1} + z^{-2} + z^{-3})(1 + z^{-4})/8 \\
&= (1 + z^{-1} + z^{-2} + z^{-3} + z^{-4} + z^{-5} + z^{-6} + z^{-7})/8
\end{aligned} \tag{17.7}$$

Thus, Equation 17.7 shows that the cascaded filters expand to be identical with an SMA. In EasyLanguage, the cascaded filters would be written as

$$Value1 = Price + Price[1];$$
$$Value2 = Value1 + Value1[2];$$
$$Value3 = Value2 + Value2[4];$$
$$SMA = Value3/8;$$

(17.8)

KEY POINTS TO REMEMBER

- An N-bar SMA can be written in an iterative form similar to an exponential moving average.
- An N-bar SMA can be written as K iterative two-element averages, where $N = 2^K$.

But Wait— There's More!

I n the Introduction, I said my goal was to revolutionize the art of trading by introducing the concept of modern digital signal processing. I hope you agree that this has led to the development of some profoundly effective new trading tools. More important, I hope that these new trading tools have given you a new perspective on how to view the market as well as how to technically analyze it. Perhaps I have even changed your perspective from thinking technical analysis is bad to thinking that it is often practiced badly. My tools address the practice of technical analysis.

Cybernetic Analysis for Stocks and Futures was written on several levels. At one level, you have been given cookbook codes for trading systems with which you can begin trading immediately. The historical performance of these systems is on par with, or exceeds, the performance of commercial systems that would cost you thousands of dollars to purchase. At another level, you have genuinely new analysis tools, such as the Fisher transform, the CG Oscillator, the RVI, and the Hilbert transform discriminator to measure the Dominant Cycle period, and unique ways to combine concepts. These indicators and automatic trading strategies view the market from an entirely new perspective and therefore augment your existing tools. I invite you to read the book again—perhaps more than once—and reach the highest level possible. That level constitutes a deep understanding of both the market and our analysis processes.

If you have read my previous book, *Rocket Science for Traders* (Wiley, 2001), you see that I address some of the same topics. I even use similar terminology. For instance, I develop an Instantaneous Trendline in Chapter 2. This Instantaneous Trendline is as close as anyone can come to nearly zero lag in a smoothing filter. It therefore represents an improvement. Since eliminating lag is extremely important to traders, the ideas put forward herein are improvements over my previous works.

As another example, the Hilbert Transform cycle period method in Chapter 9 is a substantial improvement over the three alternate discriminators I previously described. The improvement is made possible through two innovations that reduce lag in the computation. The first of these innovations is the recovery of the cycle component of the prices, which saves at least four bars of lag in the detrending operation. The second innovation is using a median filter to obtain a better estimate of the change of phase from sample to sample. The previous approaches required the multiplication of data samples. Since the data comprises both signal and noise, the multiplication produced products in the form of $(S + N)(S + N) = S^2 + SN + NS + N^2$. That is, the product now has three noise terms that must be removed by filtering instead of just one term in the original data. Filtering produces lag. Therefore, avoiding a solution requiring the multiplication of data samples reduces lag in the net result.

The Super Smoothers described in Chapter 13 are also improvements over higher-order Butterworth filters. Only after reading about regularization did I realize that the Butterworth filter consists of finite impulse response (FIR) and infinite impulse response (IIR) components, and that the FIR component could be removed, leaving a nearly maximumly flat amplitude response in the filter passband. Not only are the desirable characteristics of the Butterworth filter retained, but several bars of lag are removed due to the removal of the FIR component. The result is the Super Smoothers described.

This book is by no means the final word on digital signal processing as it applies to trading. For example, Ehlers filters are in a continuing state of research, evolution, and design. Through continued effort I hope to generate more accurate models of the market that will lead to greater profits for traders. I encourage you to join me in this quest for greater accuracy and precision. Please check www.mesasoftware.com for my latest technical articles. You can apply the tools in this book in a jillion ways to improve your own trading. For example, plot the two-pole Super Smoother and the three-pole Super Smoother using the same Period for each. You will almost immediately see a trading system jump at you from the crossings of the two lines. I look forward to hearing of your successes and invite you share the new horizons you reach in your adventures in the market.

For More Information

Research is an ongoing process for me. The latest reports of my research can be found in technical papers and Power Point seminars on my Internet site, www.mesasoftware.com.

Users of TradeStation may wish to avoid the work of keying in the code and the agony of debugging the indicators and strategies. In this case, the EasyLanguage Archive (ELA) files are available for direct transfer into your TradeStation2000I platform. The files are automatically translated when transferred into TradeStation 7.0. Similarly, eSignal users may want the electronic version of the eSignal Formula Script (EFS) codes. Your can purchase the ELA or EFS files from my website at www.mesasoftware.com, or by contacting me at:

MESA Software
P.O. Box 1801
Goleta, CA 93116
(800) 633-6372

NeuroShell Trade users can obtain the DLLs and templates for the indicators and systems in this book by contacting Ward Systems Group.

Good trading!
John F. Ehlers

Notes

CHAPTER 4

1. John Ehlers, *Rocket Science for Traders*, John Wiley & Sons, New York, 2001, Chap. 14.
2. *Rocket Science for Traders*, Chap. 3.

CHAPTER 5

1. *Rocket Science for Traders*, Chap. 18.

CHAPTER 6

1. Perry Kaufman, *The New Commodity Trading Systems and Methods*. New York: Wiley, 1987, p. 102–103.

CHAPTER 8

1. The Stochastic Indicator's name is an arbitrary "term of art" chosen by its original proponents. It has nothing to do with the statistical term *stochastic*, which is defined as a randomly determined sequence of events.

CHAPTER 9

1. *Rocket Science for Traders*, Chap. 6.

CHAPTER 13

1. Chris Satchwell, PhD, "Regularization," *Stocks & Commodities Magazine*, July 2003, p. 38.
2. *Rocket Science for Traders*, Chap. 15.

CHAPTER 15

1. Burton G. Malkiel, *A Random Walk Down Wall Street*, W.W. Norton & Co., New York, 1973–2003.

Index

Printed in the United States
122989LV00003BA/15/A